What ot … Prayer

". . . The whole book is a call to faith and action as God's life and power are harnessed through the secret of effective prayer."

Lutheran Women

"The author stresses the importance of prayer and the role of prayer in a Christian's life. In addition to discussing common questions about prayer, she identifies some obstacles to faith and gives some suggestions for overcoming these. Her belief that dynamic Christian faith is the answer to the problems, challenges, and opportunities of today's world is illustrated with brief human interest stories. Some of these illustrations are very personal, but then, prayer is personal."

The Presbyterian Journal

"Her faith in prayer was gained through experience and she writes with deep simplicity of the working of prayer in the modern world of secular forces and impersonal movements. She wants to see more bland Christians, to whom religion is little more than formality, turn into dynamic, creative Christians dedicated to God and conscious of his present power."

The Tampa Tribune

"The book combines human interest, spiritual insight and practical experience with prayer, individually and in groups. This is lively, interesting reading with never a dull moment."

Courier Express (Buffalo)

"The book will prove enjoyable for all who are interested in the experience of prayer, and helpful to those who desire to make their personal contacts with God more meaningful."

The Sun (Jackson, Tenn.)

"The title sums up in five words the theme of the book. The chapters are short and answer common questions about prayer. Written simply, yet it is so alive that you feel the author's excitement and enthusiasm from her personal experiences with the living God. It will appeal to anyone. Practical, yet related to good theology. There are many illustrations on how prayer works."

Provident Book Finder

"A practical book aimed at the layman's daily experience, *The Secret of Effective Prayer* is geared to the needs of those persons who want to know when, where, how and why to pray."

Sacramento Bee

"The treatment is Bible-based, confirmed by personal experience and the convincing testimony of others."

Standard Publishing Company

The Secret of Effective Prayer

by

HELEN SMITH SHOEMAKER

A Key-Word book

WORD BOOKS, PUBLISHER
WACO, TEXAS

A KEY-WORD BOOK
Published by Pillar Books
For Word Books, Publisher

Word Books, Publisher
Waco, Texas

ISBN 0-87680-869-0

Library of Congress catalog card number: 67-19306

First Key-Word edition—April, 1976

To all those

who through the years

have adventured

with me

in the

Fellowship of Prayer

Introduction First Edition

Books on prayer arrange themselves in various categories and classes. Some are scholarly tomes which for the layman are dry and impractical. Some are so mystical in character that only certain types of minds and temperaments can possibly understand them. Some emphasize narrow theological orthodoxies. Some are so broad and visionary that they merely promote wishful thinking, while others of a more modern version are geared down to such a low level of ideology that the Cross is left out completely and individual health and happiness seem to be the only goal.

Obviously there are many wonderful books on prayer, but still it is hard to find one that is practical enough for the average layman to utilize in his daily human experience. It seems to me that Helen Shoemaker has done an excellent job in this latter direction, for her book is geared to the needs of people who want to know when to pray, how to pray, where to pray, and what to pray. This is a usable book. For many who are familiar with various fields pertaining to the subject, it may seem too elementary. Yet I have rarely seen a scholar who knew so much about prayer that he couldn't learn from a simple manual for beginners. It seems to me that almost anyone can benefit from this approach.

I am always interested in the people who write books on prayer. What are they like? Are they people who really pray, or are they individuals who spend most of their time studying the subject rather than being deeply immersed in its practice and operation. Helen Shoemaker is anything but a theorist on the subject. She is a dynamic woman of vast energy who is constantly seeking to apply it more perfectly to her own needs and to the benefit of others.

I have watched the author organize prayer groups; her effectiveness is indeed marked. She has touched many people in the city of Pittsburgh and its environs and has brought them together in small circles for the purpose of prayer, study and fellowship. Among the people with whom she works are to be found some of those you would least expect to be interested in such a program. She has touched every kind of personality, from the rich and sophisticated to the poor and unlettered. Thus, she writes out of an experience that I know is factual and workable.

I am confident that the richness of her background as a spiritual activist will be able to communicate much to those who read her book. The book deals with Christian beginnings and personal contacts with God and one another. It does not attempt to go into the social implications of the Gospel, although they are definitely intimated. She certainly is not a woman who believes that "right thinking" and faith will solve everything. She is fully aware of the fact that prayer is only a starting point and that it must result in action—the kind of action that feeds the hungry, administers justice to the abused, and seeks to encourage righteousness wherever it is absent.

Austin Pardue,
Protestant Episcopal Bishop of Pittsburgh

Pittsburgh, Pennsylvania

Contents

PART I

PART II

PART III

PART I

There is nothing so dangerous as a Christian just off his knees.

DANGEROUS CHRISTIANS

CHAPTER 1

Taking the Prayer Offensive

Not long ago a woman voiced to me what seems to be the universal longing in the hearts of all of us:

"If only I knew how to pray," she said. "If only I could believe that prayer works as you Christians say it does."

A mother whose son is saved from threatened blindness knows that prayer works. Anyone who has experienced God's great gift of healing knows that prayer works. In answer to prayer the Holy Spirit goes into action to empower and guide doctors, nurses, parents, statesmen, military leaders—all of us.

Our most effective secret weapon against the forces of evil of this world right now is universal and continuous prayer. A spiritual renaissance among the God-fearing peoples of the world is more to be feared by evil principalities and powers than nuclear weapons. Over and over the power of God-filled men has been demonstrated to be overwhelming. The power of a faith-charged atmosphere is fear-inspiring to the forces of evil and darkness.

A young Latvian Christian who escaped a Communist firing squad by a miracle and who is now in this country, said to me wistfully one day:

"If the 900,000,000 Christians in the world knew how to pray and really prayed, we would not need to fear the power of hydrogen bombs, or the power of evil men with evil ideas, or the power of the Devil himself."

And Billy Graham said:

"The disciples did not come to Jesus asking Him *to teach* them wisdom, or how to do good. They came to Jesus asking Him to teach them to pray, and," adds Billy Graham, "Satan trembles when He sees the weakest saint upon his knees."

Prayer is a force as vital as electricity, a force that can be utilized only by those who love and trust God, and who let the stream of their life purpose run along in the stream of His great will. When we put the drop of our tiny will into the stream of His deathless purpose, we may ask anything and it shall be done for us. When we abide in Christ, our tiny will becomes an atom in His almighty will, and in His name we speak spiritual continents into being.

Jesus tells us:

"Whatsoever ye shall ask in my name, that will I do, that the Father may be glorified in the Son. If ye shall ask any thing in my name, I will do it" (John 14:13–14).

He also says:

"If ye abide in me, and my words abide in you, ye shall ask what ye will, and it shall be done unto you" (John 15:7).

And:

"For verily I say unto you, If ye have faith as a

grain of mustard seed, ye shall say unto this mountain, Remove hence to yonder place; and it shall remove; and nothing shall be impossible unto you" (Matthew 17:20).

The Man who quieted the storm, who walked on the water, who healed every kind of sickness, who brought the dead to life, who Himself stepped alive out of a tomb, told us to have faith to ask in His name. He has opened the way for us straight to the throne of God. Our password is prayer in His name.

The late Dr. E. Stanley Jones tells us:

"In prayer you align yourself to the purpose and power of God and He is able to do things through you that He couldn't do otherwise. . . . For this is an open universe, where some things are left open, contingent upon our doing them. If we do not do them, they will never be done. So God has left certain things open to prayer—things which will never be done except as we pray."[1]

Prayer, then, is "Religion in action."[2] It is love in action. It is faith in action. And it works.

It was an autumn evening. A group of young couples was drinking coffee in an attractive New York apartment. The sparkling skyline of midtown New York stabbing the warm dark night provided a perfect backdrop for the scene. On the sofa next to me sat a personable young man, a college graduate, a veteran of World War II. The purpose of the gathering was to discuss our Christian responsibility in today's world.

"I'm not a Christian," the young man said to me wistfully. "I wish I were. You people have something I haven't got, but to my way of thinking it just doesn't stand up against the facts of life."

Only a week later this young man's wife telephoned my husband to say that he had just been taken to the hospital with polio. She asked for our prayers. We held a weekly service for healing in our church, and Tom was prayed for at that service. The wife, a person of very strong Christian faith, also called some of her friends and asked them to pray for Tom daily.

He was literally submerged in prayer.

Of course he was alone in an isolation hospital. He realized fully what it would mean if he were to be crippled for life. He was just getting established in business after his long war service; he had a wife and two children to support. Why had this terrible thing happened to him? Why?

In his loneliness and fear he suddenly began to crave to read the Bible. His wife sent him one, and he read over and over the story of Jesus. He read of Jesus' healing the blind man, the lame man, the nobleman's son, and the beautiful words of encouragement seemed to be calling to him across the centuries:

"Come unto me, all ye that labour and are heavy laden, and I will give you rest" (Matthew 11:28).

"I am the way, the truth, and the life" (John 14:6).

"I am come that they might have life, and that they might have it more abundantly" (John 10:10).

As he read, both the fever and the fear began to go. His doubts began to dissolve too. He wondered why he, in his puny pride, had ever dared to say, "It doesn't stand up to the facts of life." He realized that here in a hospital room suffering from a dreadful disease, he had been ushered into the presence of a Person so wonderful and a Power so mysterious that there was nothing left for him to do but to say humbly:

"Lord, I believe, help thou mine unbelief."

A month later a pale, thin young man walked through my husband's study door. "I don't know why I came," he said. "I guess it's because I'm looking for someone to thank."

Together he and my husband knelt, and the young man poured out his gratitude to the great God who had come to him in answer to the prayers of his wife and friends.

With his wife's joyful consent, this man has gone into the Christian ministry, another witness to the power of prayer and the greatness of God.

Tom is not an isolated example. All over the world other Toms and Louises are being touched to new life and power by the hand of the great Creator because someone is praying for them.

In a gripping book entitled *God's Underground,*[3] written shortly after World War II, a Roman Catholic priest tells how he traveled in disguise into Russia, where he was told that there were millions of Christians secretly meeting for prayer and Christian fellowship. His most thrilling story is of being billeted in a KGB barracks, disguised as an Army doctor. He carried the elements of the mass with him in an aspirin bottle and an iodine bottle, and celebrated mass every evening on his bed.

One evening he had just time to throw some papers over the elements as a young woman KGB officer walked in. They sat down to talk. This young woman, who had been brought up in the anti-God schools of Russia, and had been fed from childhood on anti-God propaganda, opened the conversation by bringing up the question of religion. They talked most of the night.

The next day she brought her husband and some friends. At the end of the week eight members of the dreaded secret police were baptized into the Christian faith, and knelt with the priest for prayer, on the bare floor of the KGB barracks. Perhaps the prayer you said as you mowed the yard or darned the socks or made the beds found its destination in the hearts of these KGB officers and guided the Roman Catholic priest. Who knows?

Millions of people pray daily for the redemption of Russia and China. Our prayers must strengthen and encourage millions to continue their struggle for faith and freedom, and bring unaccounted others, as God through His servant brought the KGB officers, out of darkness into His marvelous light. What is happening in Russia and China is shrouded in mystery, but we know that God is acting, and acting with power.

Millions of people, too, are praying for a great spiritual awakening throughout the world. Behind the scenes in every nation are groups of unknown men and women praying. In the great struggle for men's minds and bodies which is taking place the people of prayer may well hold the real balance of power.

CHAPTER 2

Prayer and the World We Live In

As we glance at our world, we see whole continents in ferment. Everywhere there is restlessness, conflict, danger. There are several reasons for this.

One is the smoldering upthrust of underprivileged peoples, especially in Africa and Asia, seeking freedom and independence.

The second reason for this world ferment is that wherever this upthrust begins to show itself, the sinister hand of the atheistic Communism reaches out and stirs unrest to its own advantage.

Reinhold Niebuhr, noted Protestant theologian, spoke prophetically when he warned an assembly some years ago:

"When anyone speaks comparatively and presents the Soviet system as a possible alternative to democracy, we must insist that he has not dealt with the real tragedy of our age. That consists in the horrible evils generated by the Communist alternative to our civilization. Hell knows no fury like that of a prophet of a secular religion become the priest-king of a Utopian state. Our civilization may be faulty, but the alternative is much worse. The ramparts of our civilization contain defenses of freedom which require that we support them against this new fury."

Sir Winston Churchill, at the mid-century convocation of the Massachusetts Institute of Technology on April 1, 1949, defined the real nature of Communism with alarming accuracy and foresight:

"We may well ask, 'Why have they (the Russians) deliberately acted so as to unite the free world against them?' It is because they fear the friendship of the West more than its hostility.

"Thirteen men in the Kremlin, holding down hundreds of millions of people and aiming at ruling the world, feel that at all costs they must keep up the barriers. Self-preservation, not for Russia, but for themselves, lies at the root, and is the explanation of their sinister and malignant policy.

"These thirteen men in the Kremlin have their hierarchy and a church of Communist adepts whose missionaries are in every country as a fifth column, awaiting the day when they hope to be absolute masters of their fellow countrymen. . . . They have their anti-God religion. . . . Behind this stands the largest army in the world, in the hands of a government pursuing imperialist expansion as no Czar or Kaiser had ever done."

To the men of the Kremlin, might makes right, men are meant to be governed by other men. There is no God.

Twenty-five years ago Nikolai Lenin outlined the Communist objective:

"When the 800,000,000 of Asia unite with us, the real revolution will blaze forth."

The terrifying accuracy of this strategy is highlighted by recent events in China, Korea and now Southeast Asia.

"For the first time in history the entire population of the earth can be imperiled by ruthless men at any point on its surface. We have come into the stormy latitudes of history—the strong chance is that many now living must accommodate themselves to the prospect of living all their days in the midst of strain."[4]

A third reason for world unrest and mounting fear is the accelerating atomic armaments race, and the terrifying possibility that if World War III should break out, it could mean the actual destruction of civilization as we know it.

"Millions are fatalistic. They feel utterly powerless in the presence of forces which they can neither understand nor control. In spite of our proud achievements . . . there is a widespread sense that we are waiting for catastrophe."[5]

Added to this, we moderns are engulfed in racial turmoil and spiritual turmoil, for Protestant intellectual conceptual theologians with radical ideas and strong supports from a secular press proclaim that God is dead—that Jesus was merely a man willing to grow through encounter, that prayer is an effort to tinker with God's universe, that involvement (whatever that means) is the only thing that matters.

Of course none of this is new. It happened in the first century, and St. Paul had words for people of this kind. In the second chapter of Colossians (J. B. Phillips) he says:

"Be careful that nobody spoils your faith through intellectualism or high-sounding nonsense. Such stuff is at best founded on men's ideas of the nature of the world and disregards Christ! Yet it is in Him that God gives a full and complete expression of Himself. Moreover your own completeness is only realized in

Him, who is the authority over all authorities, and the supreme power over all powers."

This menacing world scene, then, presents a serious challenge to the courage and faith of all Christians. If we were stronger in our faith, clearer in our minds, and stauncher in our courage, we would meet this challenge head-on.

Unfortunately most Christian people are not at present singing songs of triumph. We are slowly gathering our forces and recapturing the lost power and radiance of our faith, but the frightening headlines in the newspapers and the turgid writings of some modern so-called theologians influence us more than the glorious promises of Jesus and the prophets.

We modern Christians need to turn back the pages of history and rediscover that the Christians have always outthought and outprayed and outlived the pagan world. The world needs a transfusion of faith in God and the courage to fight with His weapons. It needs exactly what small harried bands of Christians through the centuries have had—a PERSON in whom to believe, the faith to obey Him, and the courage to follow Him.

CHAPTER 3

Dynamic Faith Is the Answer

It was Napoleon Bonaparte, the terror of Europe, who said:

"There are only two forces in the world—spiritual force and material force, and spiritual force always wins." Napoleon died a prisoner on the island of St. Helena. His dreams of world conquest died with him, mute testimony to the fact that he had used the wrong weapons. Just before his death, he wrote the following, although some doubt its authenticity:

"I know men, and I tell you, Jesus is not a man. He commands us to believe, and gives no other reason than his awful word, I AM GOD. Philosophers try to solve the mysteries of the universe by their empty dissertations; fools: they are like the infant that cries to have the moon for a plaything. Christ never hesitates. He speaks with authority. His religion is a mystery; but it subsists by its own force. He seeks, and absolutely requires, the love of men, the most difficult thing in the world to obtain. Alexander, Caesar, Hannibal conquered the world, but had no friends. I, myself, am perhaps the only person of my day who loves Alexander, Caesar, Hannibal. Caesar, Charlemagne and myself founded empires; *but upon what?* Jesus founded his empire on Love; and at this hour millions would die for him. I, myself, have inspired multitudes with such affection that they would die for me. But my presence was necessary. Now that I am in St. Helena, where are my friends? I am forgotten, soon to return to the earth, and become food for worms. What an abyss between my misery and the eternal kingdom of Christ, who is proclaimed, loved, adored, and which is extending over all the earth. Is this death? I tell you, the death of Christ is the death of a God. I tell you, JESUS CHRIST IS GOD."

Twenty-five hundred years before Napoleon, a prophet of Israel, facing with unflinching courage the conquest of his nation by the great King of Babylon, looked with eyes of faith beyond that peril to a future triumph, and cried out his encouragement to his people:

"Arise, shine; for thy light is come, and the glory of the Lord is risen upon thee. For, behold, the darkness shall cover the earth, and gross darkness the people: but the Lord shall arise upon thee, and his glory shall be seen upon thee. And the Gentiles shall come to thy light, and kings to the brightness of thy rising" (Isaiah 60:1, 3).

Babylon is gone, Rome is only a memory, the kings and conquerors with their armies and banners have marched across the world stage and passed on into history, their kingdoms and empires have risen and waned and fallen. No one remembers what they said or even what most of them did, but the words of Isaiah are immortal. Only the glory of God has remained, and its radiance has spread with the centuries.

The people of God, filled with His power, literally did outlive, outthink and outpray the pagan world.

They overcame the Roman Empire's effort to destroy them, and finally won the pagan world to their faith. They were the one light of the dark ages. They kept learning, art, and morals alive when the barbaric hordes from the North and East threatened to destroy all the inherited culture of the past. In some of humanity's most turbulent days, St. Augustine, St. Jerome, St. Francis, St. Thomas Aquinas, Erasmus, Luther, and millions of other dimly remembered saints, wise men, and prophets, carried the golden thread of pure faith through the centuries down to our time. These men and women have spread the light into every corner of the world. This is the great miracle of history.

Wars cannot destroy the power of this faith, dictators cannot suppress it. It is beaten out in one spot only to burst out into brighter flame in another. Because for two thousand years in the face of every effort to "debunk" God and stamp out faith in His Son, men like Dr. John Coburn, Dean of the Episcopal Theological School in Cambridge, Massachusetts, reply with words like these:

"I believe in the God of Abraham, of Isaac and of Jacob. I believe in the God of Jesus Christ. I believe in God as the Father of all mankind," and then they act on that belief.

It might be well for evil men to study history before they try to stamp out religion and launch their campaigns of world conquest. When men make war on the living God they do so not only to the peril of their immortal souls, but their lives. The words of Jesus are still true:

"Upon this rock [of your faith in me] I will build my church; and the gates of hell shall not prevail against it" (Matthew 16:18).

History testifies that spiritual force must always win in the end, because spiritual force issues from the Lord of Life Himself.

CHAPTER 4

Some Obstacles to Faith and How to Overcome Them

Spiritual force has never won automatically, however. Those who care to take a backward look into the past will notice that there never has been a time when the great world forces were not contending for the mastery.

The people of faith always have had to establish the Christian way against terrific odds. They have been a minority withstanding and conquering pagan faiths, superstition, temporal rulers, and persecution.

Christ never promised His people the type of security that would release them from suffering, sacrifice, or struggle. No, He put into our hands His weapons of prayer, love, and power, and promised us that if we used them as He commanded nothing could withstand us.

Spiritual force, then, will continue to win and conquer the enemies of our happiness and freedom when enough people come to believe in it. There are many obstacles in our minds to overcome before we can exercise this spiritual force.

When I suggested to some friends of mine recently that powerful, continuous and concentrated prayer could save us, one of them turned to me and remarked, "Then why hasn't prayer been able to head off the last two world wars? Perhaps evil is stronger than God."

Let us face it. Why hasn't prayer been able to head off our recent wars? No dogmatic answer to this question can be made, but one answer could be somewhat as follows: Perhaps there are more of the world's people filled with fear and hatred, pride and doubt, than there are people who trust God and pray. I have already highlighted the fact that the very air of the world we breathe is heavy with fear and foreboding.

"Events justify it," you might reply.

To which one might answer: "Your accumulated fears and hatreds might possibly be helping to precipitate those events."

Thought transference has been proven. Your thoughts and my thoughts can influence the thoughts of others more than we realize. Parents have proved over and over how strongly their thoughts of fear or faith can influence their children, often subconsciously.

Is it not simple logic, then, to deduce that if the majority of the world's people are confused and fearful the state of mind of the world will be profoundly affected by it? Unless we Christians are strong enough in our faith to launch spiritual force against this great weight of dark thoughts, we will be conquered by them.

Devil-filled men know how to make capital for their own ends of the doubts and fears and hatreds of the masses, the result of which is always turmoil and war. When a person is tired and fearful that person is susceptible to disease. Revolution and war are diseases as destructive to the body politic as cancer is to our physical bodies.

Jesus showed us the way to avoid wars, but we have refused to learn from Him. He gave us two great commandments—to love God with all our hearts and souls and minds and strength, and our neighbors as ourselves.

Jesus' whole life illustrated these two commandments. He loved and obeyed God with His whole heart and mind and soul, and He loved and served people with no thought of self. He never responded negatively or resentfully or doubtingly to any situation with which life faced Him. He was all positive. In short, He was a perfect channel through whom God could act, and He asks us to be channels through whom God can act.

The second question, "Is evil stronger than God?" follows naturally on the first.

If evil were stronger than God, He would never have sent His Son to show us how to overcome it. God in His wisdom knew that evil could be defeated. God, in the person of His Son, faced the cruel facts of evil and pain and death unflinchingly for us. The crucifixion was the seeming triumph of evil, and God allowed it. The resurrection, however, was God's secret weapon and with it He triumphed by demonstrating His power to replace evil, suffering, and death with the creative force of love and life. The resurrection tells more about God and His power to overcome evil than any other event in history.

But still you are not satisfied. If God has infinite power and infinite love, why does He allow the terrible things that daily menace our loved ones and our own happiness and security? Why are there hurricanes, earthquakes, fires, famine, disease, accidents? No human being can explain the whole mystery of human suffering. The greatest minds in history have struggled with the problem of pain.

God's explanation is Jesus. He is like the shaft of light which a lighthouse throws on a black, turbulent sea. As we come into the beam of this light, through faith and prayer, we begin to understand.

God sent Jesus, not to take all the insecurity and danger and challenge from life, but to teach us to live and pray so that we might joyfully cry with St. Paul:

"This is the victory that overcometh the world, even our faith" (I John 5:4).

My husband often said, "It is not what happens but the way we take what happens" that shows the difference between a Christian and a non-Christian. Many non-believers, it is true, are valiant in suffering and trouble, but there is somehow an added radiance and confidence in those who go through trouble knowing that the Lord of Life is going through it with them.

CHAPTER 5

Faith Is Stronger Than Fear

There is a passage from St. Paul's letters that seems to have been written especially for us. We face our modern hour of peril. St. Paul and his handful of new Christians were facing extinction by imprisonment, torture, and death. Struggling as they were to hold a beachhead in the antagonistic pagan world of their day, they must often have quailed and been tempted to renounce their faith as too costly in the face of these terrifying possibilities. No doubt St. Paul got many letters from his Roman converts expressing their doubts and fears. His reply is magnificently summed up in the closing verse of the eighth chapter of Romans:

"Nay, in all these things we are more than conquerors through him that loved us. For I am persuaded, that neither death, nor life, nor angels, nor principalities, nor power, nor things present, nor things to come, Nor height nor depth, nor any other creature shall be able to separate us from the love of God, which is in Christ Jesus our Lord" (Romans 8:37–39).

St. Paul doesn't tell his frightened people to escape from all their troubles by denying that they exist. He doesn't tell them to avoid them by compromising with Rome. He doesn't tell them that Jesus will magically protect them from sorrow and suffering and danger. No! He tells them to look steadfastly at every awful possibility and to know that whatever they may be asked to go through, God will be with them to give them courage and peace and, more than that, conquering power. If nothing can conquer our spirits, then nothing can conquer us. There is nothing to fear but fear.

Let us look, in the light of St. Paul's ringing promise, at the things which might defeat us. It is characteristic of St. Paul to name the final enemy first—death. We will all die some day, either by disease, accident, or old age, or war. Death is a fact. There is no escaping it. Therefore, the way we die is more important than when we die. If only we could come to believe that "death is a physical incident through which life passes" it would be much less terrifying.

A man I knew some time ago died of cancer. He had no family and few friends. As he lay dying in the ward of a city hospital, he told my husband that he would welcome death, not as deliverance, but as the beginning of the great adventure of Life. He had not been a good man, but in his illness he had found faith and freedom from fear. The Bible became for him the Book of books because it introduced him to a God who cared, a God whom he could trust, a God who would carry him through his ordeal, as He had carried Jesus through His, into the dawn of His Easter morning.

This man came to believe St. Paul:

"That the sufferings of this present time are not worthy to be compared with the glory which shall be revealed in us" (Romans 8:18).

He lost all fear of the painful process of death by cancer. His only fear was that under the pressure of pain his courage might waver, and he would dishonor his God by crying out. His death was an inspiring going, because above all the physical agony of his dying body his spirit soared glad and free. Even dying in pain could not separate him from the love of God, or the tingling expectancy of ongoing life.

I was lunching recently with a young mother and she voiced the fear that lies in many people's hearts: "I don't fear death for myself, my husband or my child; but sometimes when I awaken in the night and think of the kind of dying it would be, should an atomic or hydrogen bomb be dropped on our city, my heart turns to water."

Many of us have husbands, sons, grandsons, who are being called into the service of our country. We would not be human if we did not rebel violently against all the awful possibilities that lie in the future. We have denied ourselves many comforts and pleasures for their sakes. They and their happiness have been our reasons for living, and now the threat to them and to all our dreams and plans lies heavy on our hearts.

Plague and pestilence, battle, murder and sudden death are thrown into startling relief by the imminence of our present danger from bacteriological and nuclear warfare, and when we kneel to pray we say, "God Lord, deliver us," with new fervor. So St. Paul's vision of victory in the eighth chapter of Romans answers the cry of our frightened hearts. Inspired words always do, if we, through prayer, can make them our own.

CHAPTER 6

What Is "Prayer," Anyway?

It was shortly after sunrise and gathered in the small Presbyterian church in a country town on the Yalu River in North Korea was the whole congregation of two hundred souls with their pastor. This was not unusual. Five to 6 A.M. is the hour of prayer in Korea, and Korean Christians are accustomed to meeting at this hour. What was unusual was that on that particular hour on that particular day of that particular year this small band of people were in dire peril of their lives. They were like all the rest of us—at certain times in our lives there is no place else to go but to our knees. The Communists had declared war on all North Korean Christians, because they knew that the Christians of North Korea were among the people who might thwart their evil designs. The news had leaked through from Pyongyang, the North Korean capital city, that the Communists were systematically rounding up, torturing and killing the clergy and scattering their flocks. Hundreds of Christian ministers alone had been killed.

As this little congregation knelt in prayer with their pastor, seeking the guidance of the Holy Spirit, it came quite clearly to the pastor that he was to tell his flock that they were to flee that very day, leaving everything behind them: their homes, their farms, their businesses, their clothing—everything that spelled their customary way of life and security—and go out in total blind obedience and trust, because God told them to.

These people believed that their pastor was a man of God. When he told them that God would go with them, that He had a plan for them, that He would save them, they believed him. They believed, with him, Jesus' great promise, "Ye have not chosen me, but I have chosen you, and ordained you, that ye should go and bring forth fruit, and that your fruit would remain . . ." (John 15:16).

Within a few hours they were on the road. The pastor divided them into two groups—one group went off with his wife and the other went with him. They hid by day with friendly folk and travelled by night. They shared all that they had with each other, especially their prayers. After thirteen months of incredible hardship—a few fell sick, a few died and were buried on the way—they found each other in Seoul. What a joyous reunion! Before they tried to find shelter or food or work, they fell on their knees, gave thanks, and again asked the Holy Spirit to lead them. He led them to shelter, the rudest kind of corrugated metal shacks, and work of sorts, enough to keep body and soul together and a few warm clothes on their backs. Most Christians would have complained over such dreadful insecurity; but not these, they were confident that God would provide. They covenanted with one another and with Him that as they went about their daily tasks, meeting the thousands of other desperate refugees who had flooded the city, they would tell the good news of how God had led them and was leading them and caring for them, and like the early Christians they added to the church daily.

Pretty soon they had doubled and tripled in number. They met together for their daily prayer in the open air or wherever they could find a roof under which to gather. And still their numbers increased. When there were one thousand of them the pastor and the elders, after much prayer, shared with the flock that they were to build a church in which to worship. Although all of the young men were in the army, there were still a few builders and carpenters in the church, and they rallied the able-bodied men to quarry and haul rock while the women dug the foundations and the children carried the dirt away in baskets. Everybody worked, everybody prayed, everybody shared with everybody else, and every man, woman and child radiated so much faith and joy in their living Lord that the news of them spread like wild fire through the city and new Christians joined them daily.

After two years the church was completed, and two thousand of them gathered together to ask the Lord's blessing. It must have been a glorious moment, and they must have had a glorious sense of accomplishment, but their trials were not over. The victorious Communist armies, swelled by thousands of Chinese, were drawing nearer and nearer to Seoul. Soon it became obvious that they were going to capture it. What was our valiant band of Christians to do—give up the struggle and say to God bitterly, "God, we have trusted You. We have obeyed You. We struggled to build this beautiful church in which to worship because You told us to. We have brought all these people to You. How can You do this to us?"

We soft American Christians might have said this, but not these apostolic Korean Christians!

They calmly faced all the odds and all the new perils in which they stood. They recalled the guidance of the Holy Spirit had caused them to leave all that they loved and knew in the North. They thanked their Lord for the way in which He had led them and loved them and prospered them, and they asked Him to show them what to do now. He did! Again they were to refugee, to Pusan this time, not two hundred but two thousand strong. Again they were promised that they would be shown what to do and how to do it and again they obeyed.

They remained in Pusan for two more years until Seoul was once more in American and South Korean hands. While in Pusan they covenanted with one another that they would not return to Seoul until each family had won one other family to Christ. They then proceeded to help their new converts build themselves a church in Pusan. They did not return to Seoul until the new church was built and consecrated.

I had the privilege of worshipping with this congregation (the Yung Nok church) in Seoul in 1961, nine thousand strong now. I heard their wonderful pastor preach. I was present when four thousand voices shook the rafters with the verses of Whittier's great hymn:

> "In simple trust like theirs who heard,
> Beside the Syrian Sea,
> The gracious calling of the Lord,
> Let us, like them, without a word,
> Rise up and follow Thee."

"How wonderfully appropriate," I thought.

And in a moment the vast congregation fell silent. Then one by one like wavelets cresting in the sea one voice after another was raised in sentence prayers. My whole being tingled with the swelling beauty and power of it. I thought to myself that this is what it should be like; this is what has given these people this dauntless courage and faith and joy. Yes, joy, for as we left the church everyone was smiling—the old men in their white coats and black shiny horsehair hats, the women in their exquisitely colored Korean dress, and the hundreds of gaily clad children. I couldn't help recalling the amazing question in the form of a promise that St. Paul put to those first Christians, "Do you not know that the saints are to manage the world?" (Corinthians 6:2, Moffatt). Saints like these—old saints with serene patient faces marked with the wisdom of redemptive suffering and defeats as well as victories; young, eager, joyous saints and lively children who were believers because their grandparents and parents had been a living witness to them of a living Christ.

Later that day a Christian friend asked if I knew what the miracle of the saints was. When I said that I didn't, he remarked:

"This is the miracle of the saints, this is their crown of glory—that every morning, despite the anguish of the night before, they rise up to resume the struggle undaunted and undismayed. They never give up."

Before my mind's eye passed all those joyful faces —"every morning, despite the anguish of the night before, they rise up to resume the struggle. . . ."

The next morning at sunrise, the church bells of Seoul began pealing the familiar hymns, and I went to the window and watched the dozens of shadowy figures leaving their tiny courtyards and hurrying to the church for their hour of prayer.

I made further inquiries about this amazing congregation. I discovered that this one church which had begun with a few worshipping and obedient souls on the Yalu River now had not only swelled to a congregation of nine thousand, but had sent thirty missionaries throughout the villages and towns of South Korea to tell the good news of the great things God had done in and through them. They had sent a missionary to Thailand and one to Formosa; they had started a radio and television program and a school for the deaf. I found out that the glorious textiles woven into the indescribably beautiful colors and designs worn by the Korean women were largely manufactured by the members of this congregation.

Here in microcosm was an illustration of the people of the living God—the true apostolic succession—from Noah and Abraham until now—those who worshipped Him and obeyed Him—those who did not turn back even when they could not see the next turn in the road—those who with dauntless faith and obedience from the first days until now have been on "mission," not permitting suffering, or danger, or hardship, or apparent defeat, or even death to deter them from their purpose.

And everywhere they have *witnessed.* This had been typical of them. One summer day an exquisite Korean lady dressed in her lovely gown of watermelon pink and green gauze, carrying a silk sunshade, was seen to cross the arched crimson-lacquered bridge which spanned a lotus pond in the grounds of the royal palace. Sitting on a bench by the lakeside with a huge basket of Korean turnips and cabbages beside her was a wizened, exhausted-looking farmer's wife, dressed in soil-stained white. The beautiful lady sat down beside her and, with a radiant smile, greeted her. The old farm woman grunted—such salutations between the high and low born are not customary in Korea. The beautiful lady kindly asked her where she was from and what brought her to Seoul. The old farmer's wife began to thaw, and it wasn't long before the beautiful lady asked, "Are you a Christian?" "Naw," replied the old farmer's wife scornfully. The next Sunday the old farmer's wife was in church with the beautiful lady, and shortly afterward she was baptized.

I expect that this story could have been repeated thousands of times when each member of this church, even as they attempted to keep body and soul together, spoke of their faith and hope to those they met during their daily comings and goings.

We are carried back through the centuries and see the small persecuted bands of first century Christians meeting secretly in upper rooms, in catacombs, behind locked doors. They had the very same characteristics. J. B. Phillips says of them, "These men did not make 'acts of faith,' they believed; they did not 'say their prayers,' they really prayed."[6] Very little of the modern church could bear comparison with the spiritual drive, the genuine fellowship and the gay, unconquerable courage of the young church.

This church in Korea is a reproduction of the gay young church of two thousand years ago.

Recently a great evangelistic campaign was launched by the church in Korea—their goal, nothing less than thirty million for Christ in the next ten years. The speaker at the great opening rally of the campaign was Dr. Han, the pastor of the Yung Nok Church.

I have told this long story because, in these days of the "golden age of science" and the apparently golden age of the conceptual and reductionist theologians with their "God is Dead" theories, it is well to be reminded that since the beginning until now there have been the "experiential" people who have believed God like Abraham, who have taken Jesus at His word when He said:

"Ye have not chosen me, but I have chosen you, that ye might bear much fruit and that your fruit would remain."

"What on earth has all of this got to do with prayer?" you might ask. "Everything," I would reply, because woven into this story like the warp in the woof of a beautiful tapestry are all of the basic principles of prayer.

What is prayer, anyway?

It is LOVE IN ACTION.

First and foremost prayer is love for God. These people learned from experience that they belonged to God—that He was their maker, redeemer and friend. They didn't know any long words with which to describe this knowledge; they knew it because their pastor, whom they trusted, told them so. The Bible, which was their book, told them so. Jesus, who was their living Lord, told them so. It probably crossed their minds that their God asked them to do some strange and dangerous things but, as He had told Joshua so many centuries ago, "Be strong and of good courage; be not afraid, neither be thou dismayed: for the Lord thy God is with thee whithersoever thou goest" (Joshua 1:9). He was telling them the same now.

And so, because they believed this about God, it was quite natural to show their love by falling to their knees in adoration and then to turn their eyes to one another and out into the world around them.

Prayer is INTERCESSION. Dr. Robert McCracken of the Riverside Church in New York says: "The prayer of intercession is the noblest form of Christian prayer, for in it love and imagination reach their highest and widest range."

And Dr. Werner Von Braun, the nuclear physicist, says, "Prayer is the hardest kind of work, but it is the most important work we can do now."

Why did this little band meet daily together at dawn for an hour to pray? They met because they knew that when they kneeled in prayer He, their Great Intercessor, was there already interceding for them so that they could come with confidence and ask Him to help them and to guide them and to protect them on their journey and, above all, to keep their courage up.

Finally, prayer is so many things, but perhaps most of all it is AFFIRMATION. Some say that the last phrase of the Lord's Prayer was not taught by our Lord but was added by the early church for those Christians who were being burned as torches in Nero's gardens, sewn into animal skins and thrown to the lions, and cut down by gladiators in the arena. In the midst of this they prayed, "For Thine is the kingdom and the power and the glory forever," the great affirmation. And so the little band of Koreans knelt every day on their tired, travel-worn, trembling knees and made together with one heart and voice the great affirmation of their faith, "For Thine is the kingdom and the power and the glory forever," before they trudged on into the unknown with joy in their hearts.

PART II

SUGGESTED SECRETS OF EFFECTIVE PRAYER

1. Personal commitment to our Lord Jesus Christ with the belief that truth is a person, that that person is Jesus Christ, and that He calls us to such a commitment.
2. That we worship God as Jesus taught us to do in the opening sentences of the Lord's Prayer.
3. That we listen for the guidance of the Holy Spirit in silent expectation.
4. That we learn now to engage in creative intercession as a result of listening for the guidance of the Holy Spirit.
5. That we repent and forgive.
6. That we pray in the name of Jesus Christ.
7. That we take time and are regular in our devotions.
8. That we learn to fast and pray.
9. That we thank God for His blessings.

CHAPTER 7

How to Approach God

"Prayer is the Sword of the Spirit," but how are we, average people like us, to learn to grasp this weapon and use it? We feel so inept when we try to pray, so ineffective, so inarticulate. Perhaps the reiteration of a few spiritual laws will help us.

If you really want to learn to pray with power, certain spiritual exercises are essential. Any potential singer knows how much time must be spent on breathing exercises and scales. Any potential golfer knows that there is no hope of ever playing good golf unless he or she is willing to spend hours practicing the drive, the approach, and the putt. Baseball players, mountain climbers, cooks, doctors, lawyers—all know there are certain rules, techniques, governing their profession or vocation. Unless they learn these techniques they will never become good singers or baseball players or golfers or doctors. And so it is with the potential pray-er.

One of the most important essentials of effective prayer is time and regularity. It is not enough to pray merely when the spirit moves us, although the spirit will move us more and more frequently as we cultivate our relationship with God.

It is not enough to treat God like a fire brigade and wait for the fire to break out before calling Him to the rescue.

If we gave as little time and regularity to eating as we do to prayer, we should probably die of malnutrition. We spend two or three hours daily at our meals, and feel very virtuous if we spend twenty or thirty minutes daily at our prayers.

A Christian should be a person to whom Jesus is a living presence. He cannot become a living presence unless we cultivate our friendship with Him—seek Him out, study the things He says about Himself and life and us. In short, spend time with Him every day. Then prayer will become a reality to us, and open doors for us which, without prayer, will never open.

A friend of mine makes a comparison with human friendship. If we value a friend, we take the trouble to keep in touch with him. We write to him, telephone him; we do things for him that we know will please him. We invite him to our home and take care not to allow any misunderstandings to come between us.

Should we be less considerate of God? He stands ready to give us much more than the love and understanding and comfort of friendship—He stands ready to give us eternal joy and absolute victory. He will not force His attention upon us; He will not force His way into our homes and hearts. Holman Hunt's great painting illustrates His attitude perfectly: "Behold, I stand at the door, and knock: if any man hear my voice, and open the door, I will come in to him and will sup with him, and he with me" (Revelation 3:20). He is there, standing at the door of our hearts, graciously waiting for us to invite Him in.

Shall each of us, then, make a compact with ourselves, to cultivate our relationship with Him? Take the trouble to rise a half hour earlier than formerly, pick up our Bible or some other book about Him, read about Him, think of Him, pray to Him? This puts us in the mood to open the door of our day and invite Him to share it with us.

It is not enough to ask Him to share our day with us, rather we should put our day and ourselves at His disposal, so that He may use us for His purposes. The very thought that He might wish to channel His greatness through our littleness fills us with awe and gratitude.

It is no accident that Jesus opened the Lord's Prayer as He did. This helps us to visualize God—in other words, know something of Him to whom we are addressing ourselves. That is why those who think of God as a vague first cause or merely as Creative Mind or the Source of all Energy do not ever understand how to approach God in prayer, as did the prophets and Jesus.

Jesus introduces us to God in one short inclusive sentence: "Our Father, Who art in Heaven." If, as the mystics agree, worship brings revelation, then the first great expression of recognition in the Lord's Prayer is the height of revelation. Here Jesus presents us to God in all His personality, His majesty and His glory.

The phrase, "Our Father," is perhaps the most hope-inspiring phrase in any language. "Our" is a great inclusive word. God is the father of us all. The whole human family is His creation—black, white, brown, yellow. He has given life to all and endows us equally with the capacity to acknowledge Him. He cherishes the life He gives. Jesus describes this tenderly when He says: "But the very hairs of your head are all numbered" (Matthew 10:30).

God's Fatherhood, if we are to believe Jesus, is a great eternal fact. However, we do not realize this until we acknowledge it. We all have human fathers, but we do not fully appreciate all that the word implies (if they are good fathers) until we consciously acknowledge them, appreciate them, honor and cherish them; then we enter into a relationship of mutual trust and fellowship, which is priceless.

I am one of those fortunates who have had a wonderful father. As a child, I took his humor and tenderness, his understanding and wisdom for granted. When I became older, however, I began to realize that real friendship is not a one-way street, it requires response. When I gave back to him, to the best of my ability, the understanding and appreciation which he had always given me, our relationship flowered into a rich unity of spirit.

Jesus used the familiar word, "father," because that word is a fact in all our lives. We understand what it should mean even if, in our human frailty, we have failed to give it meaning.

But Jesus sweeps our minds up and beyond to a further revelation of what He means by Father. He says: "I and my Father are one" (John 10:30). "He that hath seen me hath seen the Father" (John 14:9). In other words, "I am God's mirror to you. I am He in human form. If you cannot visualize Him, look at me, my claims, my teaching, my quality of life. In me you will see him."

Then Jesus adds the phrase, "who art in heaven." There is nothing written that so graphically describes the majesty of "Our Father in heaven" as the first few verses of the sixth chapter of Isaiah. As you will remember, Isaiah, the prophet, as a young man, was in the temple at prayer, when he saw a vision which he describes with glorious imagery:

"In the year that King Uzziah died I saw the Lord sitting upon a throne, high and lifted up, and his train filled the temple. Above him stood the seraphim; each had six wings: with two he covered his face, and with two he covered his feet, and with two he flew. And one called to another and said: 'Holy, holy, holy is the Lord of hosts; the whole earth is full of his glory.' And the foundations of the thresholds shook at the voice of him who called, and the house was filled with smoke" (Isaiah 6:1–4, RSV).

What a picture of the majesty and glory of God. Jesus wishes us to see this same picture, so in the phrase, "Who art in heaven," he lifts our sights heavenward, after focusing them on so familiar a word as Father.

Here is God in His universal aspect—the creator and director of the universe and of life; the fountainhead of divine energy. Mind above all minds. Wisdom above all wisdom. Power above all power. Light above all light. Love beyond all love. No wonder we fall to our knees in worship and adoration.

William Temple, the late Archbishop of Canterbury, said that "the name is the manifested nature."[7] Therefore, when we say, "Hallowed by thy name," we are revering and praising His nature as it has been revealed to us. No one has ever expressed this ecstasy of recognition more beautifully than Sidney Lanier in his poem, "The Marshes of Glynn":

"As the marsh-men secretly builds on the watery sod,
Behold I will build me a nest on the greatness of God:
I will fly in the greatness of God as the marsh-hen flies
In the freedom that fills all the space twixt the marsh and the skies."

And Archbishop Temple also says:

"The world will be saved by only one thing and that is worship."

CHAPTER 8

How to Pray with Love and Sacrifice

Jesus commands us to pray for the world before we pray for ourselves. He implied that we should do this in the first word of the Lord's Prayer—"Our." We are so human, our thoughts tend to revolve around I, me, mine, my aches and pains, my fears and worries, the aches and pains of my loved ones.

Jesus reminds us in "Thy Kingdom come, thy will be done on earth as it is in heaven," that our first duty as Christians is to identify ourselves with God's redemptive purpose for the world. Intercession for the needs of the world is part of the action of redemption. Our prayer for the Kingdom is the part we take with Him in helping the world to become the kind of place He wishes it to be.

Jesus not only prayed, "Thy kingdom come," He gave His life to establish it. On the cross the whole triumph of redemptive love over man's selfishness and self-centeredness was won, and that redemptive action is a living eternal thing. In the great phrase, "He ever liveth to make intercession for us" (Hebrews 7:25), we are given a picture of this continuing life of redemptive prayer.

It is as if He were saying to us: "I am alive. I am with you. When you kneel in prayer I kneel with you. And with me are the angels and archangels and all the company of heaven. We are joining our prayers to yours. Take heart, then. It is my will that love should triumph over hate, justice over injustice, right over wrong, truth over error. If I am for you, and all this great company in heaven are for you, who can be against you? Remember what I said to Martha at the tomb of Lazarus, 'If thou wouldest believe, thou shouldest see the glory of God' " (John 11:40).

Dr. E. Stanley Jones says, "Asking is the symbol of our desire. Some things God will not give until we want them enough to ask."[8] Our asking or intercession is the part we take with Jesus in bringing in the Kingdom. It is the highest form of creative action.

How much thought and time and discipline do we give to our prayer for others? The Roman Catholic Church considers redemptive intercession for the sins and needs of the world so important that her sons and daughters enter great praying orders like the Trappists and Carmelites and Carthusians. To these monasteries and convents go the men and women who wish to give their whole time to redemptive prayer for the world.

This is not necessary for effective prayer, however. We all can and should learn to pray as we live our daily lives.

There are several guides to effective, redemptive prayer. The first is love and sacrifice. Love is the giving of our whole heart to a cause or a person. In redemptive prayer we give our whole heart to the cause or the person for whom we pray. We lift that cause or that person up into God's own presence in confident faith that He will supply all the needs of that cause or that person according to His great power.

Phyllis, a young college girl, did this very thing. One Sunday morning a long distance telephone call informed Anne, one of her friends, that Anne's only baby niece lay dying of polio of the throat. The whole family was in a desperate state of anxiety. Phyllis' heart went out to Anne in her grief. What could she do?

She felt a strong urge to pray, so she went off to a quiet spot and poured out her soul to God for that baby. She lifted the baby as best she could, and placed her before God, asking for all His good gifts for her family. She forgot time and place and self completely in her concern for this family.

An hour or so later, she returned to the dormitory, found Anne and two other friends, and they spent the afternoon together in quiet prayer. Her faith and love were contagious—Anne began to come out of the state of grief and shock into which the bad news had thrown her. The other friends, both of whom had never prayed before, following Phyllis' lead, really gave themselves to prayer with her, and they began to have a confident feeling that all would be well.

At seven o'clock that night another long distance call came in. Anne went to the telephone, trembling and yet strangely at peace. Her friends stood around her in an eager circle. Her sister's voice was strong and clear at the other end.

"Anne, a miracle has happened—the doctors are amazed—the baby's throat muscles have relaxed and she is breathing normally. They say if this keeps up she will live and get well. Oh, Anne, thank God!"

Anne turned from the phone with the tears streaming down her face—tears of joy and relief—as she gave her friends the message. They couldn't say a word, they were overwhelmed, Phyllis most of all, that her small offering of love and sacrifice had produced such astounding results.

Fasting has always been considered a very important part of redemptive prayer. In this comfortable age, it is not considered good form to go to so-called extremes in anything. The practice of fasting, except occasionally on stated days or stated seasons of the church year, has not been encouraged. Yet fasting is a symbol of love and sacrifice. Jesus definitely implies this when He was able to heal the epileptic boy after His disciples had failed.

You will recall the occasion. He had just come down from the Mountain of Transfiguration, where, after fasting and deep prayer, He had suddenly been clothed with transfigurating radiance before the astonished eyes of Peter and James and John. Immediately upon descending that mountain He is faced with the challenge of the epileptic boy and the father's desperate appeal. As He heals the boy, He says simply: "This kind can come forth by nothing, but by prayer and fasting" (Mark 9:29).

If you are deeply concerned for some person or some cause I suggest that you fast and pray for a day or two. My richest experience of the results of fasting and prayer had to do with a dear friend who was going through the ordeal of watching a much loved husband slowly die of a series of strokes.

During this time, of course, I prayed daily for my friend—for courage and patience and faith for her, and for release and peace and abundant life for her husband. No assurance came to me, as it sometimes does, that he would be healed and live in this world. Neither did that assurance come to her, and one morning she experienced what so many of us go through at some time of our lives—that experience which

Jesus expressed for us so heartrendingly in His blackest moment on the cross: "My God, my God, why hast thou forsaken me?" (Mark 15:34). Temporarily her faith wavered and her courage gave way. She was worn out, physically, nervously, and spiritually.

I knew at once that her desperation demanded the utmost from me. No words of mine could reach her, she was beyond human comfort. Only an extra effort of love and sacrifice on my part would help, so I fasted and prayed for twenty-four hours. The next morning her faith and courage had returned.

I was with her shortly afterwards when her husband died. She was quiet and steady and tender right up to the end. As we knelt at her husband's bedside she and I both felt God's divine comfort and reassurance flowing into her and sustaining her.

These two illustrations of the power of love and sacrifice need no further explanation. They carry their own message. God knows what is in our hearts. God is love and when our hearts are filled with love, they are filled with God. Then our prayers release His full love and power.

CHAPTER 9

How to Pray with Persistence

Another essential of redemptive prayer is persistence. Many people are puzzled that Jesus put so much emphasis on persistence in prayer. He tells us to pray without ceasing, then he illustrates this with the stories of the unjust steward, the laborers in the vineyard, the importunate friend and the unjust judge. Archbishop Temple interprets these stories this way:

"We know that God does not grant petitions in order to rid Himself of the nuisance which we become by our persistence; His choice of a parallel so completely inapposite is a challenge to us to seek the real reason why God may make long delay and then grant our request. . . . The purpose of God's delay may well be to detach our faith in Him from all trust in our own judgment. Scarcely anything deepens and purifies faith in God for His own sake as surely as perseverance in prayer despite long disappointment."[9]

The wonderful Old Testament story of Jacob wrestling all night with the angel is an illustration of the importance of patient persistence in prayer. You remember Jacob's final word to God as the dawn broke: "I will not let thee go, except thou bless me. And there He blessed Jacob" (Genesis 32:26).

I have been much inspired by Florence Nightingale's dogged determination to pursue what she felt was God's call to her to go into nursing. The description of her patient struggle to overcome the opposition of a neurotic mother and sister, the Victorian taboo against careers for women, the steady, jealous antagonism of the medical profession and army brass, makes challenging and inspiring reading.

From the age of seventeen, when she first felt called to nurse, until she was thirty years of age, she steadily and patiently prayed and fought for her chance. Finally, the walls of convention and prejudice crumbled before her continuous prayer. The story unfolds as if God were directing events in such a way that the skeptical world would have no choice but to yield to her fierce and obstinate will to obey God's calling to her. The results of her persistent faith were worldwide. For, in answer to prayer, God gave her the royal power to awaken the whole of society to the need for adequate, sanitary, scientific, loving care for the sick and wounded.

If we examined the lives of those who are the trail blazers of this world—the Jeanne D'Arcs, the St. Francises, the Lincolns, the Wilberforces, the Schweitzers, the Laubachs—we would see that behind their phenomenal accomplishments lies the will to pray without ceasing, "Thy kingdom come, thy will be done on earth as it is in heaven." And, "Oh God, use me to do my small part in the building of that kingdom."

I have a friend, a middle-aged businessman, who is convinced that should the United Nations be supported by a minute of good will observed in unison around the world three times each day, tremendous things could happen for peace and that God would exercise His power to "still the rude wills of men's wild behavior."

Accordingly, in spite of indifference, skepticism and the formidable difficulty of being unable to mention the word God or Christ because of the different world religions, this man has succeeded in establishing "A Minute for Peace" at the United Nations. This is the way in which it is described:

"A revolutionary technique to meet the requirements for world peace is beginning to win support. It is called 'Minute for Peace.'

"It is based on the idea that peace must begin in the minds of men and that with conscious direction and timing, intensive prayers, thoughts of good will and peace could change the global mind from mutual fear to mutual trust.

"19:00 Greenwich Mean Time (2:00 P.M. Eastern Standard Time) is the initial moment designed for daily observance. All those who would like to unite their thoughts for peace in this special way are invited to join at this time with thoughts of love and good will for the whole family of man—adversaries as well as friends.

"Of course a 'Minute for Peace' at any time will help, but especially during *The* 'Minute' (2:00 P.M. in New York).

"Some see in this a psychological tool for brotherhood, others, a vehicle for the flow of the Spirit of God through the minds of men.

"Following are some of the ways in which you can work for peace through 'Minute for Peace.' Please check one or more:

"BECAUSE PEACE IS IMPORTANT. . . .

( ) I will telephone two or more of my friends today and tell them about 'Minute for Peace.'

( ) Each day, during my 'Minute,' I will invite my

companions to join for a moment the increasing multitude who are sending thoughts of good will and peace to heal the hatred in the trouble spots of the world.

( ) Each morning I will take time to listen to my own 'inner voice' for ideas and actions that will help build a peaceful world."

I know a woman in England, a middle-aged spinster who does not need to earn a living, who felt called by God to devote herself and her prayers to the cause of the unity of Christendom. Twelve or fourteen years ago she came to her bishop with a strange request. Bishops, like other clergy, are somewhat allergic to women with ideas—granted some of our ideas are quite wild and they have reason to be wary. However something told the bishop that this woman's request was genuine and from the Holy Spirit, and this was the request: that she be permitted to kneel in the crossing of his cathedral for three hours every day so that she might intercede there for the unity of Christendom. This was all she asked, and he granted her request with considerable amazement that any human being would want to give herself with such selflessness to such a demanding commitment.

This was all this woman was called to do, and she obeyed implicitly. When the bishop first told me about her, in true American over-activist fashion I quickly asked, "What else did she do?" He raised his eyebrows, looked at me rather critically and said, "Nothing. She was obedient to the thing that God called her to do and what do you think has happened? More than two hundred interdenominational groups have been brought together quite mysteriously all over England with this very same intention in prayer, and a large group of under-graduates in Oxford University calling themselves 'The Scares' have agreed to fast and pray every Friday for the same intention."

All this happened before Pope John called together the first Vatican Council. Her prayers were joined to the prayers of other thousands of individuals and groups, unknown, anonymous, all over the world in every communion praying for the same intention. Is it possible that the great breakthrough which is taking place in communication between the different Christian denominations could go back to this faithful obedience in prayer on the part of these unknown individuals and groups? I am one who thinks this is very possible, because our Lord impressed on us the importance of obedience and persistence, and some people have taken Him quite literally.

Thousands are unitedly praying for these intentions. There should be millions. Our prayers should roll in one great swelling wave to the foot of God's throne.

CHAPTER 10

How to Pray in Jesus' Name

Many people are puzzled by the apparent contradictions in Jesus' teaching on prayer. Close on the heels of His command to pray without ceasing comes the statement: "For your Father knoweth what things ye have need of before ye ask him" (Matthew 6:8). If God is omnipotent and knows what is in all our hearts, then why bother Him by telling Him what He already knows? Are we to try to change His mind? Can we persuade Him to alter the course He has charted for us or for someone else? Isn't it part of His plan that a well-rounded life must know sorrow as well as joy, struggle as well as peace, pain as well as power? I believe that Jesus solves this dilemma for us in His last great teachings on prayer in the Gospel of St. John.

"And whatsoever ye shall ask in my name, that will I do, that the Father may be glorified in the Son. If ye shall ask any thing in my name, I will do it" (John 14:13, 14).

"And in that day ye shall ask me nothing. Verily, verily, I say unto you, Whatsoever ye shall ask the Father in my name, he will give it you.

"Hitherto have ye asked nothing in my name: ask and ye shall receive, that your joy may be full" (John 16:23, 24).

Archbishop Temple interprets these verses as follows:

"When the condition mentioned is satisfied, our wills are identified with the will of God; we are then praying for what He desires to give and wants to give until we recognize Him as its source. . . . This means that the essential act of prayer is not the bending of God's will to ours, but the bending of our wills to His. The proper outline of a Christian's prayer is not, 'Please do for me what I want' but 'Please do in me, with me and through me what you want.' "[10]

Therefore, alongside of persistence we must place trust in God's love and God's plan. We need to make our own the great assurance of St. Paul: "All things work together for good to them that love God" (Romans 8:28).

This is not the negative resignation by which we so often interpret the phrase, "Thy will be done." It means, rather, the creative, joyous confidence that in His will lie life and peace and joy, no matter how dark the immediate state of affairs.

This in fact is to pray in Jesus' name.

A simple story illustrates this great truth. A year or so ago a friend wrote to me that Mrs. N., a close friend of hers, had fled to New York to get away from a desperate personal trouble. She was praying that Mrs. N. would come and see me. A few days later, Mrs. N. telephoned. She sounded like a person in deep distress. I invited her to lunch and she accepted. I found that she was a very pretty, beautifully groomed middle-aged woman, obviously well-to-do, but, oh, so unhappy.

Over our tea and salad, she poured out her personal tale of woe. She had been married to an alcoholic. For years she had given up pleasure, friends, social life, in order to devote herself to helping him. In the end he had been cured of alcoholism, but not of his weakness for women.

One day he came home and calmly informed her that he was leaving her. Not a word of gratitude, appreciation, affection, or even apology was offered. Mrs. N.'s whole world caved in. She felt rejected, humiliated, and bitter. She had literally fled to New York, away from the sympathy and well-intentioned advice of her friends and relatives. She had taken a hotel room, and, with the aid of sleeping pills, was nursing her grief. Her head was in a whirl, she knew no peace —what was she to do?

After she had poured it all out, I suggested that we go and kneel in the church, and pray about it. She looked up through her tears and read these words written in gold under a beautiful stained-glass window:

"In the world ye shall have tribulation: but be of good cheer; I have overcome the world" (John 16:33).

Suddenly she realized that here lay her answer. She was carrying a burden of sorrow and frustration that God wished to lift from her shoulders. Then and there, kneeling at the altar rail, she first gave Him her fear, her resentment, her sense of humiliation, and, finally, her husband. She relinquished her burden and trusted that God would fulfill His promise.

You see, Mrs. N. had been demanding that God give her husband back to her; in other words, "God, give me what I want." The result was the despair I have described. As we knelt at the altar she was able to say,

"God, I want what you want; whether my husband and I come back together lies with you; meanwhile I will trust you fully."

It was then she began to know peace and the sense that God would lead her into happiness and usefulness and a new sense of dignity and self-respect. This He has done in abundant measure; she has become one of the most loved and creative members of her church and community. God's power re-created her spirit when she relinquished her burden and her will.

God is the Master Weaver. He has created a glorious design for this world as the great tapestry designers did in the Middle Ages, but He depends on us, His people, to follow His design as He has outlined it on His drawing board.

We weave the tapestry with the threads of praise, persistence, trust, love, and sacrifice. Like the ancient weavers, we weave from behind, obediently following directions on His blueprint, and as we weave, the great design takes shape and gradually stands out clear and complete. It can happen to us; it can happen to others through us; it can happen to our world—if we trust Him and pray in His name.

CHAPTER 11

How to Ask for Forgiveness

One condition of all powerful prayer is emphasized by the phrase, "Forgive us our trespasses as we forgive those who trespass against us." Unless our attitude toward God is repentant He won't hear us. Unless our attitude toward others is forgiving and redemptive, He won't hear us.

It is no accident that the Episcopal Church sets aside forty days each year for fasting, penitence and prayer in order that we may examine ourselves and prepare our hearts and minds for the glorious experience of Easter. Jesus' forty days in the wilderness were just such a time of self-purification.

So with us. God has given us the gift of prayer. Prayer is spiritual dynamite. We cannot use it to satisfy self-interest and personal ambition or merely human desire. We need a constant cleansing of our inner attitudes.

Recently a friend put this alarming question to a group of complacent Christians: "How would you like to remain in the room if all your thoughts were projected on a silver screen with the title: 'One Hour in The Thought Life of Helen Smith Shoemaker, or Mary A. Randolph, or Priscilla B. Yates'?" We laughed, but our mirth was uneasy.

In the Book of Common Prayer there is a prayer called the "General Confession." This prayer is said in preparation for Holy Communion. It is a very disquieting prayer. We say this:

"Almighty God, Father of our Lord Jesus Christ, Maker of all things, Judge of all men; we acknowledge and bewail our manifold sins and wickedness, which we, from time to time, most grievously have committed by thought, word and deed, against thy Divine Majesty, provoking most justly thy wrath and indignation against us. We do earnestly repent, and are heartily sorry for these our misdoings; the remembrance of them is grievous unto us; the burden of them is intolerable. Have mercy upon us, have mercy upon us, most merciful Father; For thy Son our Lord Jesus Christ's sake, forgive us all that is past; and grant that we may ever hereafter serve and please thee in newness of life, To the honour and glory of thy Name; through Jesus Christ our Lord. Amen" (Anglican Book of Common Prayer).

Many people say to me, "I don't like to say the General Confession, because I really don't feel it necessary to 'bewail my manifold sins and wickedness.' I do not feel very sinful or very wicked. I do not grievously commit sin 'by thought, word and deed against His Divine Majesty.' I don't really believe that I 'provoke his wrath and his indignation against me.'"

If a poll were taken, most of us would agree that the General Confession is overdone, the language too archaic for modern Christians. It all seems an exaggeration. We have been going to church, many of us all our lives; we have been saying our prayers regularly, we have been trying to live by the Golden Rule, we are neighborly and bighearted, and generous. We are conscientious wives, husbands, parents; we are trying to be honest in business. How, then, does it apply to us?

It applies to us very directly if we identify ourselves with all Christian people. When we think of saying the General Confession for the Christian people in the world, as well as for ourselves, and taking our share of the blame for the compromise in the Christian Church, it puts matters in a very different light. As we look at the world around us we cannot be very proud of what we members of the Christian Church have accomplished in bringing in the Kingdom for which we pray every time we say the Lord's Prayer.

When we look at the corruption in public life—both state and national—when we look at the racial and national prejudice still rampant in the world, when we consider the very unpleasant fact that one out of every twelve people in the United States is either neurotic or emotionally or mentally confused, when we see the drug addiction, the sexual excesses, the mounting crime in our cities, it doesn't make us feel very effective as Christians, does it? If we were more vital, if we were more dedicated, if we were really channels of God's holy power and energy, these conditions would not continue to exist, and Communism would have no appeal. If the Christian Church were a pillar of fire leading the peoples of the world, instead of an ambulance corps, bringing up the rear as it so often seems to be, Communism probably would not have been born.

So much for our share in the guilt of all of us as a so-called Christian nation. What about our personal guilt? What about our personal sin? A great many of the things that we consider sin are the result of partial commitment, partial trust, partial dedication.

Gossip, criticism, pride, intolerance, prejudice, hatreds—these are the symptoms of sin, not sin itself. If sin is anything that keeps us from God or another person it shows itself in all these reactions.

One symptom of a half-dedicated life is self-centeredness, touchiness and credit-snatching. I meet women constantly who are unhappy in their church group. They say that the other women in the church are cold and snobbish or try to wall off newcomers. They feel lonesome and insecure and unwanted. Often they either continue to come with a chip on their shoulders or leave and go to another church, only to discover that the same conditions exist there. Or they stop going to church altogether, stating as their reason that the church is so full of hypocrites that they cannot be bothered with it.

What these people need to do is to search their own souls to see if the fault does not lie partly in themselves. The church has never claimed to be a society of saints, but rather a fellowship of sinners, each of us imperfect but each of us trying to pattern his life more nearly on His whom we come to church to worship.

Another symptom of a half-dedicated heart and soul is prejudice. Many of us feel that because we are Episcopalians or Baptists or Roman Catholics, that, somehow, we are superior to all other Christians. Others of us feel that because we are Christians we are superior to Jews, or because we are white we are superior to blacks.

A young wife whose husband is with our AID Program in East Africa writes home to her mother:

"Our image abroad has been perpetrated by people who make unwitting remarks in front of people that they don't think are listening. I heard an American woman say at the yacht club the other day, 'Why I told my dog that he was ugly as an African and just as dumb.' And we expect people to be grateful to have us here! You can bet that the waiter who was standing right there took it all in and spread the word to the people who lived near him."

"Every act of racial discrimination or prejudice in the United States is blown up by the Communists abroad, and it hurts America as much as an espionage agent who turns over a weapon to a foreign enemy. Every American citizen can contribute toward creating a better understanding of American ideals abroad by practicing and thinking tolerance and respect for human rights every day of the year." So said Richard Nixon on his return from a state visit to Asia.

I have mentioned several symptoms of a partially dedicated life, national complacence, self-centeredness, and prejudice. Search your own soul for the others and put pride, both national and personal, at the top of the list. Then get down on your knees and ask God to forgive you. When you have done this, offer your prayers and He will hear you.

CHAPTER 12

How to Pray for Those Who Sin Against Society

Let us now turn from "forgive us our trespasses" to the other side of the coin, "as we forgive those who trespass against us."

Peter came to Jesus and said, "Lord, how oft shall my brother sin against me and I forgive him? till seven times?" Jesus replied, "I say not unto thee, Until seven times: but, Until seventy times seven" (Matthew 18:21, 22).

Earlier He had told his disciples, "For if ye forgive men their trespasses, your heavenly Father will also forgive you: But if ye forgive not men their trespasses, neither will your Father forgive your trespasses" (Matthew 6:14, 15).

One of my audience at a school of prayer was very much disturbed by this statement. It sounded like tit for tat to her. She didn't think God was a revengeful God. We had a long conversation about it. He is not a revengeful God, but when we refuse to forgive our brother his trespasses, we block the stream of His power. We set up a barrier between ourselves and God so that His power cannot flow toward us. We do this, He does not. He does not revenge Himself—He is not that kind of a God. He merely allows us to cut ourselves off from Him by our wrong attitudes.

There is a legend that Leonardo da Vinci, when painting "The Last Supper," painted the head of his enemy on the shoulders of Judas. That night he could not sleep. The following day he was to paint the head of Christ, but every time he tried to see the face it blurred. So after another sleepless night he got up, went to his studio and erased the head of his enemy from the shoulders of Judas. Immediately he saw the head of Christ clearly.

There are three attitudes that we can take toward those who have sinned against us and those who have sinned against society. We can condemn them, we can condone their sins, or we can redeem them.

One can easily see that condemning does not get either those we condemn or ourselves anywhere. It leaves us sitting in a nice little pool of self-righteousness. It bars them out of our prayers and out of our lives. Neither does condoning get them or us anywhere. That it too sentimental.

"Forgiveness is not supine," runs a quotation. "It is a beneficent invasion. It is alert and patient and creative."

Our forgiveness of others must be like God's forgiveness of us. He has so much to forgive us. He is so gracious and patient with us that we can hardly be less alert, patient and creative toward those who have wronged us.

First, shall we apply this principle to those who have sinned against society? How shall we pray for them? We can condemn them. If we do, we cannot pray for them. We can condone them and excuse their sin, or we can redeem them through prayer. Our prayers can become the beneficent invasion which seeks to draw them away from their wrong attitudes and actions into the ways of God once more. Justice demands that the Hitlers and Stalins and Maos of the world pay the penalty for their deeds, but mercy seeks to redeem their hearts and souls. Is that perhaps the proper attitude to take?

In an article in the *Saturday Evening Post* a Lutheran chaplain assigned by the United States Army to the Nazi war criminals during their trial in Nuremberg reports that being a Christian, he knew that if the thief on the cross could repent and be redeemed in his death agony, it was possible that even a Nazi war criminal might repent and die in a state of grace. So the chaplain offered himself as God's channel to these men and because of his redemptive love he won the confidence of even the most hardened. With one or two exceptions, they made confession and received absolution before their deaths. Justice demanded that they pay the full penalty required by international law for their crimes against society, but because one man's prayers and one man's attitudes were completely redemptive God used him to seek and save that which was lost.[11]

The story of this chaplain's action has helped me in my attitude towards world leaders whom I feel are evil. For a long time I could not pray for them. I felt that their crimes against humanity and against God had been too great for them to receive the notice of any decent person's prayers. Then I remembered that they were lost souls if ever there were any. If Jesus came to seek and to save the lost, could I, His follower, do less?

Several times I have attended funerals of people who have broken every rule in the book—men and women who have been belligerent agnostics, alcoholics, libertines—unrepentant to the end. Their loving relatives have seen to it that they had beautiful Christian funerals. I often wondered how the minister could read the glorious words of the funeral service with any sincerity for such people, and yet he does. When he comes to that tremendous passage, which I have already mentioned in this book—the last passage in the eighth chapter of St. Paul's Epistle to the Romans, one suddenly understands:

"For I am persuaded that neither death, nor life, nor angels, nor principalities, nor powers, nor things present, nor things to come, nor height, nor depth, nor any other creature, shall be able to separate us from the love of God, which is in Christ Jesus our Lord" (Romans 8:38, 39).

So that is it. No matter what we do or not do, God never gives us up. His love follows us into this world and through our lives and into the next world. We can repudiate Him and break His laws and hurt our fellow men and ruin our own lives and still He loves us, not sentimentally, tepidly or supinely, but with a strength that in the end will not be denied.

We cannot flee Him, the doers of evil cannot flee Him. He will catch up with us all some day, somewhere, and we will turn and fall on our knees before Him. For He is God and God is love.

There is a sin mentioned in the Gospels and the Epistles, the sin against the Holy Spirit, which we are told will not be forgiven. What that sin is, is shrouded in mystery. It may be the denial of God; it may be such repeated flouting of His great law of love that the man or woman who does it is consigned to perpetual outer darkness. It could be calling God bad, as the Pharisees did when they accused Jesus of casting out devils by the Prince of Devils. It is not for us to judge this! "Vengeance is mine; I will repay, saith the Lord" (Romans 12:19). It is for us to throw our prayers into the breach wherever there is a chance that a soul may be salvaged by them.

CHAPTER 13

How to Pray for Those Who Sin Against Us

It is easier to pray for those who have sinned against society than for those who have sinned against us personally. I doubt that there is a single individual reading this book who has not been sinned against, or does not feel that he or she has been sinned against by someone. What are we to do about these people who have sinned against us? Are we going to try to avoid them—wall them out of our thinking and our lives? That may be possible, but it is no solution. What if one of these people lives in the same house with us?

There are thousands of mothers with rebellious children, thousands of wives with unfaithful husbands, thousands of children with problem parents.

I know a widow who has laid down her life for her son. She has refused remarriage, she has earned the money to put her son through school and college. She has loved and nurtured him with great care and great self-sacrifice.

Apparently the boy has not appreciated all this. He rebelled and at the first opportunity he left her and went off on his own. He has not attempted to repay her or support her in any way for all the years of self-giving. What is the mother to do? She can condemn, or she can condone his conduct, or she can redeem this son. She has chosen the third course.

First, she has examined herself to see where she may have failed. She has discovered possessiveness, and a demand for appreciation and thanks, which has put an emotional pressure on her boy which he could not or would not meet. Then she discovered self-pity and "How could he be so cruel to me?" attitudes in herself. Lastly, she found that she had indulged and protected him through his childhood so that he was not equipped, either emotionally or spiritually, to meet life's demands.

This woman is a brave woman. She has faced her own faults in this relationship and asked forgiveness for them. She has not blamed or resented the boy's conduct, rather she has put him into God's hand, patiently praying and believing that he will find God's plan for his life and his future. Meanwhile, she is continuing cheerfully to earn her own living and make her own life. That is living and praying redemptively.

Through the years I have watched one of my closest friends restore an unstable, alcoholic husband to normalcy. She has patiently stood by him through the temperamental instabilities of his early effort to break the habit. She has given up her own very successful career in order to further his. She has sought in every way possible to create the kind of relaxed, beautiful home to which he would want to return. He has been irritable and rebellious, self-centered in turn, but her love has held firm and her confident faith that he would find the way has triumphed over every set-back. He has found the way and become not only a good husband but a successful member of society.

We hear a great deal today about prodigal parents and I have been amazed at the patience, long-suffering and maturity of some people's children.

I have a young friend who illustrates perfectly the difference between condemning, condoning, and redeeming a very difficult family situation in which she was caught. When she was very young her father divorced her mother. The child was given into his custody. A year later he married another woman. The other woman decided to show the world she could bring this child up as a lady. Her pattern of behavior was to treat her very much as the stepmother treated Cinderella. Diana was not allowed to go out in the evening, not allowed lipstick or pretty clothes; onerous household chores were given her.

The only matter the stepmother could not control was the child's love for the church and her desire to go there. It was undoubtedly God's love and power that the girl experienced in the church fellowship that gave her the steadiness to remain alert and patient and creative in the midst of her personal ordeal.

When she was seventeen her father's eye began to wander once more, and the stepmother went to pieces emotionally. After a time of prayer, Diana knew the time had come to challenge her father. She hated to hurt him, as she loved him, but she realized that if she could prevent it she could not allow him to disrupt any more lives.

So she gathered her courage and went to his office. She talked to him straight from the shoulder. He denied everything, but she countered with, "Daddy, I am sorry, but I know what you are doing. You helped to wreck one home and now you are preparing to wreck another. For all our sakes you will have to change your ways." It was very direct, very simple, very loving. There was something about her—God in her perhaps—that the father could not deny. After a time of great turmoil and conflict, he came around. He and the stepmother were reconciled.

God's reward to this wonderful child was the rediscovery of her own mother. Diana had been kept away from her mother. It was probably just as well, for during the eight or ten years when she did not see her mother, the latter, who had been a very weak and self-indulgent woman, got hold of herself, repented of her shortcomings, and found a rich, strong faith of her own.

It may have been due to Diana's believing prayers, for during those years of separation she told me that her love and prayers and yearning for her own mother grew steadily stronger. The moment she was of age she went and found her mother again. Their reunion must have been very touching for she wrote about it so joyfully:

"Mother's been finding what I have been finding, possibly as a result of our prayers, and the wonder of it is that our two hearts have met in a greater love."

I met a woman recently who had one of the saddest faces I have ever seen. She was a widow. She had been widowed for some time. One day she asked if she might talk with me. After some preliminaries, she burst out, "You know, I simply can't get out of my heart my hatred for the man who I feel was the cause of my husband's death. My husband knew that he was both dishonest and irresponsible, but he hoped to change him by kindness and patience. The strain and anxiety of the whole situation caused the stroke that killed my husband. I cannot shake off my hatred for this man. I used to be interested in the church and all kinds of civic affairs, but I can't concentrate on anything any more. Nothing interests me—I feel so lost and desperate."

We talked a long time. I told her about the many imaginary conversations I had held with myself about other people, wanting to get even, wanting to give blow for blow, wanting to have the last word, until I realized that how other people behaved to me was not my business but God's. My only concern was to treat others as God treats me.

As a result of our talks and prayers together this woman began slowly and painfully to pray for the man whom she felt had killed her husband. As she began to understand what "redemptiveness" meant and became redemptive, her whole life was transformed. She who had been lost and desperate came back into the stream of God's love.

The most difficult people to forgive are the people who resist us, those who resist our will. Have you ever felt frustrated and angered by somebody who continually resists you?

For instance, if you are religious, if you believe in saying your prayers, if you like to go to church, and your husband or your child or your mother or your father does not, what do you do? Many people come to me and say, "I'm just boiling with resentment. I can't get my husband to say his prayers or go to church. He won't do anything I want. Wouldn't you think he might do it to please me?"

One of the worst sins of wives is wanting our husbands to find their way to the Lord our way, exactly our way, and to persist in tugging them along like lagging children. Many women have complained to me about this and I reply, "Pray for your husband and really live like a Christian at home, and let him grow his wings his way. One day he will come to church on his own initiative."

Do you have trouble forgiving yourself? Over and over and over do you blame yourself? If you do, try to remember that God loves you, that God loves you much more than He judges you. He tries to bring us to see our sins, yes, our failures, and things we do to put up barriers between ourselves and other people and Him. But the most important thing about God is that He loves us. He is not trying to punish us. He is trying to draw us to Him, so that He can use us as His channels. We block the channel when we fill it with self-blame and inferiority and continual self-scrutiny. We must trust ourselves to God's love as we trust ourselves to the water when learning to swim. Just as we cannot learn to swim if we thrash and struggle in the water, so we can never learn the greatness of God's love unless we take Jesus' word and trust ourselves to Him.

A woman of my acquaintance has a daughter who has miserably failed as wife and mother. She is weak, self-indulgent and self-centered. The mother has been overcome with self-blame and an overwhelming sense of failure and guilt. She is not helping her child by taking this attitude. She has been a woman of real Christian faith, but has allowed her sense of guilt and self-blame to become obsessive to the point where it is like a black cloud blotting out the sun.

Finally, there are those of us who need to forgive God. How many there are who, under the shock of great personal tragedy, turn from God and His Church with the bitter words, "Why has this happened to me? What have I done to deserve this?" When we do this we retreat from every possibility of healing or comfort. In our self-centered grief we reject the verdict of history, of the millions of people who have put their hands into the hand of God when it was night so that He might lead them into the dawn.

One day recently, after a talk on forgiveness, a lovely-looking woman came up to me. She said, "The last thing you said about 'forgiving God' struck me. My son, a pilot, has been missing in South Vietnam.

I asked God bitterly, 'Why should it be my son?' and He gave me an assurance which dispelled my bitterness and has stayed with me through all these months, that wherever Kim is, he is in his Father's keeping and is fulfilling his destiny. I just know that God is watching over and using Kim. I wish I could share this assurance with all the bitter, grieving mothers."

Jesus placed at the very heart of His perfect prayer: "Forgive us our trespasses as we forgive those who trespass against us."

CHAPTER 14

How God Guides Us

We modern Christians need to recapture the vivid sense of the Living Presence of Christ in the person of His Holy Spirit. The early disciples took Jesus' promises about the Holy Spirit in St. John's Gospel quite literally. The first ten chapters of the Book of Acts are a vivid record of how God, through His Holy Spirit, guided the first Christians in establishing Christianity in the Roman world.

What did Jesus tell us about the Holy Spirit? Some church leaders feel that a comma should be placed after "Lead us" in that phrase of the Lord's Prayer, "Lead us, not into temptation." They say that Jesus intends to refer to the guiding power of the Holy Spirit. One ancient version of the Lord's Prayer puts it this way, "Lead us, lest we fall into temptation."

Jesus is very specific in describing the role of the Holy Spirit. First, the Holy Spirit is to be a counselor. Second, He will make the truth plain and give courage to follow it. Third, He will be in us. Fourth, He will teach us. Fifth, He will remind us of Jesus' teaching and His commands. Sixth, He will guide us and give us foresight. Seventh, He will give us power.

So, in a nutshell, Jesus introduces us to the Holy Spirit. The doctrine of the Holy Spirit tells us that God is very close to us—nearer to us than breathing, closer than hands or feet. Therefore, He is continually seeking to communicate with us. "Only because it is God's nature to reveal or communicate Himself is there a world at all. Everything in it, every single occurrence in time or space, is subject to this controlling fact, that the world exists as the arena of God's self-revelation."[12]

God revealed Himself in all His glory to us in the person of Jesus. He is still seeking to reveal Himself to us through the Holy Spirit, who is the Living Spirit of Christ.

In his book *Conversion of the Church*, my husband reminds us of the central importance of listening for the guidance of the Holy Spirit. He says, "Religion today is largely the imitation of an example when it ought to be the hearing of a voice. And so the interior life of Christians has become a dynamo, busy with plans and philanthropies and activities, when it ought to be a receiving set primarily concerned with catching the messages from on high." Does that fit any of us?

To a person puzzled about Divine guidance a humorous British friend wrote a postcard. On it he drew a man's face with two big ears and a small mouth. Underneath he wrote, "You have two ears and a small mouth. Why don't you listen twice as much as you talk?"

Whether it be in personal prayer, or group prayer, or even in our great services of public worship, a time should be set aside for silence and listening. When we telephone a friend we do not do all the talking and then replace the receiver before listening for his reply. Prayer is not a one-way street. We do not travel up it to a dead end. No, in prayer we go up the street to meet God and He comes down the street to meet us. Out of that meeting and the counsel and direction He gives us comes our action in building His Kingdom.

There is a story that one day an Episcopalian was invited to a Quaker meeting. The congregation sat together in silence so long that the Episcopalian grew restless and whispered to his Quaker friend, "When does the service begin?" to which the Quaker replied, "The service begins when the meeting ends." This may be the secret of the extraordinary effectiveness of the rather small Quaker group. They wait together in silence until the inner light of the Holy Spirit illuminates them unitedly, then they act with power.

In the tenth chapter of the Book of Acts is told the story of how the Holy Spirit, through guiding two men, changed the course of history. One of the men was a Roman centurian. Apparently this man, like many Romans, had been profoundly affected by the Jewish belief in one God. He prayed to God as the Jews prayed, and one day as he was praying for more understanding God's Holy Spirit came to him in a vision and told him to send his servants to Joppa and find a man called Peter, who would enlighten him further. The Roman did not question his vision, as we are apt to do. He obeyed and immediately sent his servants on their errand.

The other man was St. Peter. St. Peter was praying on the housetop of a friend and he saw a vision of a great sheet let down from heaven and in it all manner of creeping things and four-footed beasts. A voice said: "Rise, Peter; kill and eat."

Peter was not as quick in his obedience as the centurion. He questioned the validity of the vision. All his Jewish training and prejudice rose up in resistance. No pious Jew would consider eating any meat that was not kosher. It was considered mortal sin. Again the voice said: "What God hath cleansed, that call not thou common." Peter was not yet convinced. He was not sure that this might not be a temptation. Possibly he recalled the phrase in the Lord's Prayer, "Lead us not into temptation," and hesitated lest this be false guidance. As Peter hesitated, the three servants of Cornelius knocked on the door of the house and asked for him. While they were knocking the Holy Spirit spoke to Peter again: "Behold, three men seek thee. Arise, therefore, and get thee down, and go with them, doubting nothing; for I have sent them."

Peter stopped questioning and obeyed. The men took him to Cornelius' house. Cornelius had invited all his friends and relatives to meet and hear Peter. You see, Cornelius was so sure Peter would come that he was all ready. Peter, introducing himself, told them how unlawful it was for a good Jew to meet, or associate in any way with, non-Jews. "But," he concluded with amazement, "God hath shewed me that I shall not call any man common or unclean." He proceeded to tell them all about Jesus, and as he reached the climax of his story, the whole company was visited with a united sense of the presence of the Holy Spirit.

This story illustrates perfectly the sevenfold action of the Holy Spirit. He counseled with Cornelius and Peter as they prayed. He sent an angel to speak with Cornelius and appeared in a dream to Peter. He made the truth plain to Peter in his dream. He gave both men the courage to obey His guidance. He filled Peter with grace and wisdom as he spoke to Cornelius and his friends. He reminded Peter to tell them of Jesus' teaching. He gave Peter foresight in his dream. He released His power into the whole company when Peter had finished speaking.

This event, perhaps more than any other in history, marks the establishment of the Christian church in the world. If Cornelius had not obeyed, the good news about Jesus might not have been carried to the pagan world. If Peter had not obeyed, it is quite possible that Christianity would have remained a Jewish sect. There was a very real chance that Peter's intolerance and prejudice—the result of the traditional exclusiveness of the Jewish people—might have overruled the guidance of the Holy Spirit.

It is startling to us to realize that the course of history was changed by two men's obedience to guidance. It is still more startling to us to realize that the building of Christ's Kingdom often depends on just such obedience.

This great truth was put to me very simply years ago. "God has a plan. You have a part. Find it. Follow it." How wonderful that each of us can have a part in carrying out God's plan. Unless we learn to listen for the guidance of His Holy Spirit and obey Him, we will miss our part.

Possibly that is what is wrong with the world. So many people miss their parts—either through indifference or unbelief, or just plain disobedience. That is the reason why prayer is so vitally important. It helps the people for whom we pray find God's way and their part in it. It also helps us to find God's way and our part in it.

Recently in a small church in a small suburb of a large city a tragedy occurred. The same kind of thing has undoubtedly happened in many churches throughout our country. But the way in which this possible tragedy worked out to the glory of God and toward the redemptive fellowship offered a family in trouble, as well as the redemptive action toward a teenager in the family in distress, is a superb illustration of the way in which God guides us if we will only be obedient. This story was told to me by the wife of the minister of the parish, and she and her husband were instrumental in salvaging a situation that could have torn the parish apart and brought disrepute to the church in that particular suburb. I'll tell the story in her own words:

"Tom (pseudonym), a sixteen-year-old lad in our parish, with some other teen-aged boys, committed an offense, involving criminal vandalism in a high school which seriously involved them with the law. The case was under the authority of the Juvenile Courts and the boys were placed in the Juvenile Detention Home until the time of trial. Their act brought the school system, teachers and pupils of the city under attack and judgment. The circumstances surrounding the situation were of such nature that public opinion was aroused and hostile pressure groups were brought into action. Efforts were made to influence the authorities to send the boys to the State Reformatory. This was their first offense at law-breaking and in the Juvenile Court.

"Tom had been reared in a home with a strong church background. In fact, he attended Church School regularly all his life and was active in the youth program at the time of this event. His father is a successful business man, and the family lives in an upper-class neighborhood with many social and cultural advantages. These facts spurred the desire of some groups to make this an example case for all juvenile delinquents.

"The members of our parish had a compassionate concern for Tom, his suffering family, as well as for the other boys and their families in the midst of this tragedy. This caused much soul-searching and self-examination in our personal relationships to this boy and we asked ourselves where we as a church had failed him. Various families began looking into their own homes and their relationships with each other. Even the young people began thinking in terms of the dangerous temptations around them and their needs and responsibilities to themselves and friends. The question was frequently asked: 'What can we do to help this boy and his family in the present tragedy?' It was ultimately recognized that prayer was something which all could do; that it was our mutual responsibility to join hands in prayer and surround the families and all concerned in the welfare of the boys.

"A parish prayer vigil was arranged and held in the church in which sixty people participated. Mothers, fathers, small children, young people, golden age members, all shared in the vigil hours. The families of the accused ones also came for a period of prayer. Results?

"Many who participated in the vigil expressed gratitude for the personal spiritual experience of their moments alone with God. The decision of the Judge at the time of the trial was no surprise to those who joined hands in prayer. Tom was paroled to his parents for a designated period and sent out of the state to a selected military school. At present he is becoming rehabilitated and adjusted and is happy.

"In searching for answers for the cause of the behavior of these high school students, the parents and teen-agers of our parish met to discuss the matter. The need for a meeting for teen-agers in this area was realized, a place where they could come together for wholesome fellowship and fun. Such a place is not provided in this exclusive section of the city. So the teen-agers of our parish decided to venture out and, with the support of the rector and parents, open a youth Canteen in the parish house—meeting on Saturday nights. All young people of this section of the city are invited. The young adults in the parish are acting as sponsors, and the young people attending pay a nominal fee to cover the cost of operation. Parents from the neighborhood have visited the canteen and offered their personal and financial help in continuing the project. This has supplied a need in the community and has also been a stimulus to the youth of the parish. Their joy over seeing a project come alive, their fellowship in working together and their renewed interest in the church brings rejoicing. Our hearts are humbly grateful not only for the teenagers' service to the community but for the rehabilitation of Tom.

"One cannot put a finger on any one individual incident in this story as a decisive factor. All doors were opened and God used pastor, people, the Christian judge, the school, the troubled families and the offenders to bring hope out of despair, forgiveness out of guilt, emptiness into creativity in the young people, peace and joy into the hearts of the troubled family and redemption to Tom. As the father of the boy said: 'Joy and humble gratitude now fill our hearts that were once filled with fear and despair.'

"Thanks be to God!"

This can happen in your town, it can happen in your block, it can happen in your family—if you learn to listen for and then obey the guidance of the Holy Spirit.

CHAPTER 15

How Prayer Helps the Sick

Dr. Norman Vincent Peale says this about creative prayer:

"Personally, I believe that prayer is a sending out of vibrations from one person to another and to God. All the universe is in vibration. There are vibrations in the molecules of a table. The air is filled with vibrations. The reaction between human beings is also vibration. When you send out a prayer for another person, you employ the force inherent in a spiritual universe. You transport from yourself to the other person a sense of love, helpfulness, support—a sympathetic, powerful understanding—and in this process you awaken vibrations in the universe through which God brings to pass the good objectives prayed for."[13]

A well-known writer on atomic science, the late Dr. John O'Neill, told a group of church people, of which I was one, that many atomic scientists—through purely scientific experiment—had come to the conclusion that all energy was vested in the Godhead. Atomic energy was merely a part of this total energy. Vast amounts of spiritual energy are waiting to be released.

Jesus knew how to release spiritual energy to a phenomenal degree. He healed all kinds of sickness by direct spiritual means and He told us that we could do even greater works than His if we learned to channel this spiritual energy as He did.

When He told us to pray, "Deliver us from evil," Jesus faced the fact of destructive forces in nature as well as the fact of destructive forces in human nature. The last great phrase of the Lord's Prayer is the glorious affirmation that God holds the key to the conquest of evil.

At its best, that has always been the faith of the church. Therefore, the application of direct spiritual power to sick bodies and minds—indeed to a sick world—is not only scientifically sound, but actually essential.

Again to quote Dr. Peale: "We are learning that faith properly understood and applied is a powerful factor in overcoming disease and establishing health."[14]

Many people have rejected the idea of spiritual healing as crackpot, indulged in by the lunatic fringe, and therefore not to be dabbled in by conventional and regular churchgoers. In the past few years, however, outstanding bishops and clergy in our various communions have come to believe differently. Prayers for healing as well as sacramental services for healing are now once more held regularly in some of our most orthodox churches. The laying on of hands and anointing with holy oil is again made use of as a means of healing grace.

In the early days of the Church, when little was known about medicine, surgery, drugs, and psychiatry, there were special and very beautiful prayers and services for the healing of the sick of body and mind. The Anglican Prayer Book contains many such prayers. On page 308 are special prayers for the sick. On page 320 there are prayers to be said in connection with anointing and the laying on of hands. On page 321 is a short service for Holy Communion for the sick.

Those of us who believe in direct spiritual healing feel that our doctors and scientists have been privileged to discover many effective material and psychological ways in which to heal body and mind. We are grateful for all these advances in material medicine and gladly make use of them. Through the years deeply dedicated and unselfish men and women in medicine have done much to promote bodily health and long life. We feel, however, that the discovery of so many material ways to heal disease does not afford any good reason to discard the direct spiritual healing of disease. Material means and spiritual means of healing should go hand in hand. Both are scientific.

A very fine, conscientious woman said to me, "I'm afraid of spiritual healing. I have a relative who is crippled; if I assured her that she could be healed through prayer and she wasn't, I would have raised her hopes and then dashed them. She would never believe in me or prayer again. I prefer to trust to the doctors; they are doing all that science can do and they do not raise any false hopes." People like this need the assurance that we who believe in spiritual healing do not wish to repudiate doctors and psychiatrists. We are grateful and wish to work with them. We believe God guides their efforts, as He guides ours through prayer.

A person is divided into three parts, spiritual, mental and physical. We can fall sick in any one of these three parts of us. There is a spiritual despair known as the "dark night of the soul." There is mental darkness and depression and confusion, and there is bodily illness. Any one of these can be induced and aggravated by disturbance in either or both of the other areas of our being.

All of us have experienced acute sorrow, tension, or frustration in our lives. Many of us have experienced severe physical suffering. There are times when we feel that it all adds up to darkness. That is why those words in St. John's Gospel are so comforting: "The light shines in the darkness, and the darkness has not overcome it" (John 1:5, RSV). Let us try to keep this promise in mind as we attempt healing through prayer. We can pray this shining hope into people's bodies and minds and souls. It is one of our most glorious privileges as Christians to do so. We can learn to pray, singly and together, with the kind of hope Jesus had, with the kind of faith Jesus had. I believe we are intended to pray like that; I believe we are intended to see God's living power lighten darkened lives. If we have not had that experience we have not lived. We may not be unusually gifted, but all of us can pray with faith, for the gift of prayer is offered to us all.

Illness of body is very concrete. It fills us with fear and pain. God stands ready to free us from fear and release us from pain. Two radiant friends of ours called long distance from Toronto recently to say that they had just been privileged to be a part of a group that had been used to heal a man of leukemia. Think of that! These men are not crackpots. One of them is a well-known clergyman. One of them is a prominent business man. And they had actually seen this marvelous thing take place and be checked by the doctors.

I had a rich experience last autumn in connection

with the healing of a child when I was visiting some dear friends in another city. These people were great believers in prayer. During my visit they told me of a niece whose little boy had had a tragic accident the spring before.

One morning, while the mother was telephoning in the adjoining room, the two-year-old baby climbed up on the electric stove in the kitchen. The burners were all turned on and he had burned his feet and legs dreadfully before his mother had been able to rescue him.

All that summer the doctors hoped that with the help of modern burn treatment his legs would heal by themselves. The young mother, during the hot weather, changed the bandages every day, but the legs did not heal.

Finally, in August the doctors suggested skin grafts as a last resort. At the end of two weeks the bandages were removed but the grafts had not taken. As the young mother has said to me since, "When I looked at his poor little legs and saw the great blisters where the grafts should have taken, and realized that the doctors had done all they could and that he might never walk again, I felt near to madness. I didn't think I could stand it. I didn't believe much in prayer, I didn't believe much in anything, but I knew Aunt Grace and Uncle John did, so I called them to pray very specially." (It was during my visit that the young mother called.) "Aunt Grace's reply over the telephone was to say quietly, 'I have been praying for you, but there is someone visiting me who believes greatly in prayer. Tonight at ten o'clock we will pray together for you and the doctors and the baby. Will you please join us? We will lift up your baby into God's light and we will ask that the skin grafts will take.'"

So that night we met, the aunt and uncle, my

daughter, who was with me, her fiance, and myself. There we truly experienced Jesus' promise, ". . . If two of you shall agree on earth as touching anything that they shall ask, it shall be done for them of my Father which is in heaven. For where two or three are gathered together in my name, there am I in the midst of them" (Matthew 18:19, 20). Our unity of spirit that evening was like an electric current. We were given the deep assurance that all was well. Before I returned home, Aunt Grace told me the baby was recovering.

Two weeks later I received a letter from a strange young woman. I had never thought to ask Grace her niece's name. I knew only that she and her husband were two attractive, young marrieds who lived in a near-by suburb. Life was busy and good to them, and they did not bother with church or prayer or religion until this accident to their little boy. As I studied the envelope, I recognized the postmark as that of the suburb in which Grace's niece lived. The note inside was very moving. It read:

"I don't know how to thank you and Aunt Grace for what you did after I asked for the prayers. The skin grafts took and the baby is going to be all right, and, what is more, I completely lost that awful feeling of despair, and I knew that everything would work out. My husband and I hadn't thought much about religion before, but I want to promise you, Mrs. Shoemaker, from now on we are going to be steady and devoted members of the church."

She and her husband have made good their promise and have not only gone to church but have become one of the leading young couples in that church.

In this case the need of the young couple linked to our united prayer of faith released God's healing power into the body of the child as well as into the minds of the desperate parents.

I have often been asked, "What about the times when we pray for healing and the person is not healed? Is there something wrong with our faith when this happens? Or perhaps we are fooling ourselves and prayer is only some sort of autosuggestion, which sometimes works and sometimes does not."

There are many reasons why prayers for healing seem at times not to be answered. One is that though we pray, our fear and anguish are stronger than our faith and we block God's power. The kind of prayer that is qualified by this reasoning is not much of a prayer. "Oh, God, if you can heal, please do," or, "I'm afraid this is too much even for you, but please help my sick friend." Or maybe even though we do not articulate our doubts, all the while we are praying we feel such fear and despair that our faith flickers like a candle in a heavy draft, and if the person for whom we pray dies, our faith dies with him.

This is not prayer, this is merely the projection of fear and anxiety.

Prayer is confident faith that we can bring our sick friends before God. It is confident faith that He loves them—that His will for them is that they may have life, the kind of life and light and joy and well-being that is in Him.

In the next chapter I shall tell several stories of how He gives that light and life and joy and well-being, along with complete healing of the body, as well as with partial healing of the body, and sometimes without healing the body at all.

We human beings are so willful that unless our prayers are answered in exactly the way we visualize them being answered we often fail to see the answer when it comes. The people of true prayer are those who can see the answer when it is given in God's way, not theirs.

CHAPTER 16

How Prayer Frees Us from Fear and Despair

The greatest triumph of faith I have ever witnessed happened to a friend of my husband's and mine. This story is particularly rich because a cancer was arrested after God had first released my friend from fear. Mrs. R was the able secretary of an outstanding minister. She was a wonderful and dedicated woman. And for some mysterious reason—who knows why?—good and wonderful people sometimes are called to face the most severe tests.

Many years ago Mrs. R had a breast operation which was highly successful. Years later she went to the doctor for a biannual routine checkup. After taking X-rays and studying them, the doctor called her into his office and said, "Mrs. R, I hate to tell you this, but these X-ray slides show that you have cancer in both lungs and in the bones of your chest. Ordinarily, a person with this trouble lives about six months. I am confident we can make you comfortable, but I cannot give you any hope."

She managed to get back to her apartment, and the first thing she did was to kneel down by her bed and ask God what to do. It came to her very clearly that she must come East and seek another diagnosis from the doctor who had performed the first operation.

The doctor in New York was less blunt than the doctor in the West. He indicated the X-rays might show trouble from an old bronchial condition, but he was afraid they confirmed the cancer diagnosis. He assured her, however, that he would give her the very newest treatment to check cancer.

She came to us to recover herself, to find her bearings again, to get ready for whatever the future held. Bishop Pardue says a wonderful thing to people facing death: "You are fortunate to know ahead, because you have time to prepare yourselves for the wonders of the after-life. So many people are given no time to prepare themselves."

At that time I was meeting every week with a small prayer group. We were not a group that had been meeting very long. Most of us were young in the life of prayer. I shall never forget the morning Mrs. R joined us and, at the end of the meeting, requested us to remain a moment, as she wished to ask a favor. Then she told us what she was up against and asked for our prayers. There is great power in standing in a circle and holding hands when there is some terrifically intense and urgent need for prayer. We stood in a circle that morning and we lifted Mrs. R before God with all the power we could summon, asking that she would be freed from all fear, and that He would give her light and peace.

She stayed with us a few more days and we had further prayer together. Then she went to visit her son. From there she wrote that she slept sixteen hours a day for two weeks, after which she returned to work, completely free of fear and determined to keep going as long as she could. Her letters for the next two years tell the rest of the victorious story.

January:

"You have received my wire telling you of the results of my latest X-ray and the fact that the lung cancer is positively arrested, and the X-ray is better than the others. The hormone injections will be continued, however, as that seems wise.

"As I left the doctor's office all I could think of was 'Great and Glorious Are the Works of the Lord.' And then followed the thought that I shall have a longer time in which to work for Him. There is so much to do, and so very many people hungry for a faith and an inner conviction.

"As I am writing I recognize the utter change in one's values, and the tremendous gain in inner strength when one has, with God's help, attained complete freedom from fear, as He helped me to do through His grace, and power and love expressed from all the prayers that were being said for my healing."

June:

"Helen, dear Helen, how wonderful this change that God makes in our lives! With the dread word 'cancer' one is first humanly filled with shock and creeping fear, but one day—quietly God enters in—there is a sudden realization that all fear is gone—God has 'taken over' and will carry on the rest of the way."

January, a year later:

"I have offered my services at any time to the doctor in the event he should have a patient in partial shock following a realization that he or she has cancer. I know I will be able to restore morale and witness for our Lord at the same time.

"Now I have been asked to lead the adult Bible Class of one of our new missions. There are seventy-seven families, all of them have children, young parents who are educated and very articulate, full of a desire to learn. They asked the bishop if he could get me to lead them. . . . Through a feeling of inadequacy I would have refused the responsibility had I not gone through this recent experience, which has so increased my feeling of obligation to our Lord.

"I started last Sunday. There were twenty-nine adults in the class, eleven of whom were men, two of them doctors. Of course I knew God was with me, but I have such a human lazy tendency to lean on someone else and listen to them and there I sat with twenty-nine people looking at me, pleasantly expectant!

"Everything about my life since July, 1947, has been so amazing, thrilling, and dramatic! If anyone thinks that trying to be a Christian and to grow spiritually is dull, they just don't know.

"The doctor checked me again yesterday and I'm well. Keep me in your prayers, please!"

Two years later, in July, Mrs. R had what seemed to be a return of cancer symptoms. With the same joyous trust she submitted to further treatment and again the X-ray showed the disease to have been arrested, with a further deepening of her trust and gratitude. Not only this, but she is constantly in touch with other victims of cancer, sharing her faith and courage with them. In August of that year came Mrs. R's most recent word:

"Some day science will find a sure cure for cancer, but certainly I can demonstrate a real faith which dissipates fear and raises the morale and helps to hold cancer back. . . . The treatment is based entirely on the spot shown on the X-ray. The spot on the right lung remains encapsuled and arrested."

This glorious story reads like the New Testament

—the victory, the power, the joy, the outreach into other lives that God gave to Mrs. R. First she was delivered from fear, then from all preoccupation with her disease, and lastly she was filled with such radiant light that she became a channel of that light and life to others. This woman, who was told she would live for six months, lived for seven long years of self-giving and gratitude.

Despair is an illness of the mind that always yields to prayer. Many people lead lives of quiet desperation. Too many anxieties, too many family crises, too many successive sorrows, too many responsibilities, or a long, discouraging illness often crack an otherwise strong and positive spirit.

One of the most loving and powerful Christians I know broke down under just such a series of pressures some years ago. He went South to recuperate. Rest did not help him, recreation did not help him. The kindness and advice of friends and doctors failed to reach him. He found himself floundering helplessly in a black pit of despair.

One day he flung himself down on his bed utterly defeated and overwhelmed. He faced once more the basic cause of his despair—there was mental instability in his family. It came from his mother's side. His dear brother, who had been a stable and steady citizen his whole life, died in a mental institution; three of his cousins had committed suicide. What chance had he against such powerful odds? The verdict of his whole family background was against him.

Then, like a tiny crack of light in a black room, crept the thought that some people in his church back home were praying for him. Suddenly the conviction blazed into his mind that God loved him, that Christ was that very moment interceding for him. Therefore defeat and despair were completely contrary to God's will for him. He lay quietly under the impact of this thought until it grew and grew, filling the room with light.

He got up from that bed a completely new man, and the sense of God's love never left him. We knew no one who radiated God's love as this man did. He was permeated with it, and he released it into every life he touched. Hundreds of alcoholics, neurotics, and even the most hardened criminals owed their restoration to him. When God calls such people to Himself, they seem to be merely moving on into a richer fulfillment.

A woman of fifty, the wife of a minister, who for years had had perfect health, and was a superb complement to her husband in all his work, was taken ill with a virus infection of the middle ear. She was a deeply dedicated woman, perfectly disciplined and selfless. She believed in healing prayer and prayed with some of the best-known leaders in spiritual healing; still her body was not suddenly healed. Perhaps, like Mrs. R, she has received a greater gift. A recent letter from her tells what has come to her in this trouble:

"I could write a book about the last year and a half, and what I believe about gradual healing as perfectly possible, as well as the sudden kind. What I have already learned with ups and some downs of great discouragement and despair has been that in spite of an ear which rings incessantly, when I am close to Christ nothing can keep me from hearing His voice; in spite of the fact that I still can stand for only a few minutes with any comfort, I can stand up for Christ wherever I am, and with people He wants helped; in spite of eyes which still can be used only an hour to read or write—that is, at one time—I pray that my spiritual vision will continue to grow and keep pace with

Christ's plan. All in all, I am grateful to be alive, grateful that I can do a little more than a year ago, grateful that so many doors are opened that might be closed. I don't know, and no doctor seems to either, whether I will be completely well or whether there is permanent injury to a nerve or something.

"Last May I faced what I have as a permanent handicap—something that may never be changed. The acceptance of that brought great peace. The important thing above all else is whether I can live on top of this condition or get defeated by it, due to very frustrating limitations. I know that if I abide in Him as He tells us to, I not only can live above it, but will live above it."

This woman, as she said, has not only learned to live with her liability but to live above it. Since the writing of this testimony she has been used in marvelous ways to spearhead a prayer group movement in her own diocese, to train hundreds of women in the leadership of prayer. She has been appointed by her bishop to be the principal architect of an annual prayer group conference in her diocese. She has indirectly brought into being hundreds of prayer groups, and she has been made the chairman of a prayer subcommittee on prayer and worship in her diocese. This is truly an instance of the overcoming power of Almighty God when we dare to trust Him fully.

One of the things that makes Good Friday the deepest and most wonderful day of the Christian year is that then Jesus Himself went down into the black pit of despair for us. When we face our own Good Fridays of fear and despair we remember, too, His final words: "Father, into thy hands I commend my spirit." His last word was a word of trust and love, and God vindicated His trust and love with the triumph of Easter morning.

Easter was not only an event in history. Easter is the triumph of faith over fear, despair and discouragement. It means the revival of our souls and the rebirth of hope and courage. The people whom I have just described have experienced this revival and this rebirth.

CHAPTER 17

How Prayer Helps Those in Sorrow

Jesus faced the fact of death as he faced the fact of evil. If we are to pray compassionately and helpfully for those facing death or those in intense sorrow we need to understand better what our faith teaches us in regard to death and life.

Our prayers for the comfort of those in sorrow and those facing death often seem not to rise above the ceiling because we ourselves think of death as the ultimate enemy rather than the gateway to life. We think of it as separation from all the dear familiar places and associations and people which spell our earthly security. We think of it as walking out into the night, alone and naked, with no light to guide us. We think it writes finis to our dearest relationships. It is something we shrink from with utter dread.

This attitude toward death is totally unchristian. In almost every word and act Jesus sought to dispel it.

He said, "I came that ye might have life and have it more abundantly." On Easter He not only walked out of death into life, but out of apparent defeat into final victory. Here He demonstrated His greatest claim: "I am the resurrection and the life: he that believeth in me, though he were dead, yet shall he live: and whosoever that liveth and believeth in me shall never die" (John 11:25, 26).

It is this great fact He is asking us to believe and transmit to others. In other words, He is saying, "Trust me, trust my love for you. I am alive, I am praying for you. When the time comes for you to join me, I will call for you and you will come. At that time you will truly live, not subject to the aches and pains and problems and limitations of your life on earth, but free to exercise every gift of mind and personality I have given you. In this life there will be no bodily disease to hamper you, no selfishness, no pride or lust for power to block the growth of your personality, no limiting actions of other people to warp or frustrate the full development of all your gifts, no slavery to temptations of the flesh, no subtle poison of self-deception. Abide in me while you are on earth. I have shown you the way, so that when you come to me over here you will abide with me always."

As He has opened the gate of life to us, so He asks us to open it to others.

A wonderful old friend of mine, Mrs. M, was visiting in a hospital one day. As she entered the elevator a flurried-looking nurse pushed a young man in on a stretcher and said tensely to the elevator boy, "Operating room, emergency, please."

The young man on the stretcher looked terrified and my old friend leaned over him and smiled at him tenderly. He grasped her hand and gasped: "Lady, do you pray?" She nodded. He held her hand very tightly and closed his eyes, "I don't know any prayers," he mumbled, "and I'm so scared I might die."

So there in the ascending elevator Mrs. M prayed very simply that Christ would surround the boy with His love, take the boy's fear, and give him His peace. The elevator reached the operating floor, and the nurse wheeled him away with a grateful backward look at Mrs. M.

The following day Mrs. M was again at the hospital and as she walked down the corridor the nurse of the day before caught up with her and stopped her. She put her hand on Mrs. M's arm. "Thank you for what you did yesterday," she said simply.

"Oh, I'm so glad you sought me out," replied Mrs. M. "I came today hoping to find you and hear how our boy got on."

"He's all right," replied the nurse. "Before he went under the anesthetic he said, 'Tell the lady it's all right, I'm not afraid any more, because God is here.' That was the last thing he ever said, because he died on the operating table."

I have often asked myself whether I would have been as alert and ready to share my faith as Mrs. M was with that needy, dying boy. Almost no day passes in which we do not have an opportunity to encourage or comfort or help someone. And not an hour passes when our prayers cannot open the gate of life to someone somewhere.

The following letter describes better than I can what prayer can do to uphold a person in deep sorrow. This woman came from a fine and intelligent agnostic family. Until trouble struck her she had no faith in a personal God or personal Saviour.

Her first husband died after a long illness, her second husband died suddenly many years later, and her youngest son was killed in Korea. Through these ordeals she has found a depth and understanding and a greatness of soul that I believe few people find. My husband and I were with her at the time of her second husband's death; he was a member of our vestry at Calvary Church, New York, but we were on the other side of the country when her son was killed.

We phoned her on the day the body of her son was brought home from Korea. He had been a brilliant young flyer, one of the heroes of World War II. Yet he was used again in Korea because they were so short of pilots out there. After the burial service she wrote as follows to us:

"I was sustained all day by the Presence. And I know He was there. Perhaps I would have been fully conscious of the Spirit if I had not been thinking of your prayers and human understanding and longing to help, but I don't think so. It seems odd that in hours so terrible one goes into a world far beyond any human help or comfort, stark, staring, alone and suffering. When there is only one possible strength to turn to, you are forced to turn to Him, for there is nothing else.

"If I were what I would call a convinced atheist, I am sure I would have to do that. And to me it is the final proof there is a God. You simply are forced to turn to Him, and I am sure that there has never been a soul in the finality of his own death, or that of those who are closer to him than himself, husband or child, that has not done so.

"But what I meant when I started saying, 'It seems odd,' is, it is when you are alone there with only God you then become suddenly conscious of others, of human beings, friends, as I did at the grave, and at the very last seem to feel around you all the prayers of your friends over the past months. What an extraordinary sensation!"

It was true that a number of us had held her steadily in prayer for months, and during this time we threw almost a cordon of prayer around her.

Two other dear friends lost their only daughter, a college student, in a fearful motor accident. In a beautiful appreciation of their daughter, the father tells of the way in which God has interpreted to them their daughter's going:

"Nancy's witness for Christ always amazed me. It continued wherever she went, although at the same time she entered into all good times and was so often 'the life of the party.'

"In high school she became an outstanding leader, and at college last autumn was elected president of her freshman dormitory, and through it all she influenced so many for good.

"Just as I write this a letter comes from a college friend saying, 'Whenever I had a problem I'd go to Nancy. She'd listen to my petty troubles with interest and we'd hash it out, and before I knew it I would forget them and everything would be fine. She was always so understanding.'

"Our daughter is not dead. She lives. I know she is closer to me now than ever before. She walks with me and talks with me, and it is a wonderful joy to have her with me always.

"When I conduct a burial now, I find myself saying silently, especially if I know the person hasn't been a very good practicing Christian: 'Nancy, someone else is coming over who needs help!'

"Furthermore, Nancy lives on in the lives of her high-school classmates, who started a memorial fund for her in the high school. And she will live on in the lives of the students who shall come after her, for each year a member of the graduating class who is chosen as the student 'who has shown the most concern, interest, and love for fellow students during the high-school years' will receive a special scholarship award in her memory. . . .

"She is living on, too, in reconciled lives—lives restored and uplifted because of her life, and especially because of her death. For instance, there is the high school boy who was always somewhat dejected and retiring, whose changed expression gives evidence to the truth of what he said to me the day after the burial service, 'Something has happened to me; I'm different. Nancy's death has made me think for the first time in my life. I know what she believed and I believe it now, too!'

"She lives on, especially in our family, as we continue to serve God. Nancy had been asked to sing at the wedding of one of her best schoolmates. Her mother sang in her place, although it was only two weeks after the burial. And her mother continues to play the organ, direct the choir, and teach all of her piano pupils. It hasn't been easy; there have been many tears, but I know there is an inner peace that passes understanding.

"Yes, she sparkled with joy all her life and I believe she will continue to sparkle as she goes on to perfection. If there is a band in heaven I am sure she will have it out to welcome us on that great day of reunion when God says our work in this life is finished.

"On the headstone we shall soon erect on the beautiful spot overlooking the Hudson where she is buried will appear St. Paul's words to the Colossians: 'Christ in you the hope of Glory.' "[15]

In October, 1963, my husband died. How does a Christian family face the death of a loved one, especially a loved one who is at the same time their spiritual leader and head of the house? We are not an exceptional Christian family; perhaps our one advantage is that we were united in our love for and faith in our Lord Jesus Christ and were united in our belief in the power of prayer and His power to bring us through this experience with victory and understanding.

When Sam was very young, he wrote a poem entitled "A Prayer in Bed." It reads:

Dear Lord, one day
I shall lie thus and pray
Stretched out upon my bed,
Within few days or hours
Of being dead.
And I shall seek
Then for the words to speak,
And scarce shall find them,
Being very weak.
There shall be hardly strength
To say the words if they be found, at length.

Take, then, my now clear prayer
Make it apply when shadowy words shall flee;
When the body, busy and dying,
May eclipse the soul.
I pray Thee now, while pray I can,
Then look, in mercy look,
Upon my weakness—look and heed
When there can be no prayer
Except my need!

Our younger daughter Nickie, in facing valiantly her father's death, describes it as follows:

"At the end, a phenomenon occurred which must happen in many families when a parent becomes ill. The man on whom I had depended so completely came to depend, in part, on me. His illness was so severe as to demand some pretty constant care on the part of my mother and Mamie (our housekeeper) and myself, and my greatest joy (although it was a constant sorrow that he needed it at all) was to be able to return a little of the tremendous amount that he put into me. We sat and talked for hours and hours that last summer, and I took care of him alone for a bit when my mother had an important church obligation to fulfill. He trusted me completely with his health during that time, to give him his medication, and most of all just to be there to talk to. I've never forgotten that. I felt I had the responsibility of taking care of the most important person in the world.

"More than all the rest, I must say that for me my father is very far from dead. His memory is crystal clear in my mind, the things he said, the belly laugh, the twinkling eye, and the sickness. But more than that, he is around every corner I turn. For everywhere I go I meet people, all sorts of people, endless numbers of them it seems, that he has helped. They have read his books, he led them to Christ, he got them into the ministry. How could a man be dead who helped so many people? And also I find that as I wend my way forward in the Christian life, I turn more and more toward the way he did it. Eminently practical, this father of mine. It works, by gum, it works. It is contagious, and the same sort of religion he devoted his life to selling, and I never feel far from him because I want to sell it, too. And so, in many ways for us, 'death has no more dominion.' "

Everybody came from far and wide for the funeral. The church was jammed. Beloved Don Wilkins came all the way down from Pittsburgh and played the organ and the vested clergy who attended the funeral came in procession behind Jack Scott, the assistant minister of St. Thomas who acted as crucifer, singing "Jesus Christ Is Risen Today." It was glorious. At the end of the service we all walked out to the churchyard singing "For All the Saints" at the tops of our lungs —Nickie with her head up and the tears streaming down her face.

Our daughter Sally wrote from Korea: "My darling Mother, how wonderful to hear your own voice last night, and how wonderful to know that our beloved Daddy is gone to be with his Lord. Think what a joyous time he must be having. Court was reading last night after you called that marvelous passage from Revelation 7 about the great multitude from all nations and kindreds and people arrayed in white standing before the throne praising God forever and ever. What a glorious promise! As terribly as we are going to miss him, at this point I can only feel gratitude that God has taken him home, and gratitude that He will continue to look after us even as He has taken care of Daddy. Meanwhile, my Darling, we are with you in spirit every second of the day knowing that God is there. Give our Nickie a hug and tell her that our prayers are with her, too. At choir this week we're singing, 'I heard the voice of Jesus say, Come unto Me and rest. Lay down, thou weary one, Lay down thy head upon My breast. I came to Jesus as I was, Weary and worn and sad. I found in Him a resting place, and He has made me glad.' Korea is nearer Heaven than America. All my love, LaLa."

What we, and these people have experienced, is a grace not our own. We have known the soul strength that comes through the fact that in our darkest hours we are upheld by the love and prayers of those "who are for us" in both worlds. I say in both worlds, for I firmly believe that "those we have loved long since and lost awhile" are constantly watching over us from the other world. They know our fear and pain and human despair. They know, because they too experienced these things in their earthly life. Now, freed from these limitations, they join their prayers to the human prayers of those who love us here, so that together we may walk forward into the life to which Jesus blazed the trail.

PART III

Again I say unto you, That if two of you shall agree on earth as touching any thing that they shall ask, it shall be done for them of my Father which is in heaven. For where two or three are gathered together in my name, there am I in the midst of them.

MATTHEW 18:19, 20

And they continued stedfastly in the apostles' doctrine and fellowship, and in breaking of bread, and in prayers.

ACTS 2:42

CHAPTER 18

The Power of United Prayer

It happened in the Parish Hall of Calvary Church, New York, which had just been decorated with six or eight large posters of white elephants rampant, in preparation for a white elephant sale the following day. Tonight it was packed to the doors with three hundred people at a "Faith That Works" meeting, at which laymen spoke of their experience of faith at work in their daily lives.

As I prepared to come downstairs (we lived on the top floor of our parish house), the telephone rang. I answered rather impatiently, for I was late. It was Anna, one of our young adult leaders. She was very much upset.

Alice, her roommate, had just been rushed to a large city hospital, desperately ill with internal hemorrhages. The doctors were giving her transfusions, but were not sure they could save her. I asked how it happened. Anna didn't know. She had come home from work in answer to a phone call from Alice and found her alone and apparently bleeding to death. She said Alice hadn't seemed well that morning and when they separated for work, Anna had suggested that she come home early.

I reassured Anna, told her one of the clergy would join her at the hospital immediately, and rushed downstairs. All the way down in the elevator I kept saying, "God, what shall I do, how can I help?"

Suddenly it came to me. Alice was the girl who had painted all the white elephants which were dancing so gaily around the walls of our parish hall. I would ask the group in the hall to pray with me for her healing.

Fortunately, I found our young assistant minister in the front hall as I stepped out of the elevator. I told him what the situation was, what I planned to do, and dispatched him to the hospital.

I squeezed into the back of the hall and sent a note up to my husband, who was leading the meeting, and he called me to the platform. As I mounted, I pointed to the white elephants cavorting on all sides of us and said, "Do you like these white elephants?"

The crowd nodded and smiled. I told them why they were there and continued, "That girl who came down here and spent her day off doing them is lying at death's door in the operating room of one of our city hospitals this minute. She is an orphan, just one of the pretty talented girls who make a living in this city. There is no one to pray for her except us and a few friends. Will you pray with me for her?"

We bowed our heads—all three hundred of us. I cannot remember what I said, but I felt as I said it as though three hundred pairs of hands lifted that lonely child with me, and held her steadily and unitedly before God. Then there was a moment of deep, united silence. The meeting went on. I returned upstairs to await another phone call from Anna. One half hour later it came. All was well, Alice had turned the corner and would live.

A few days later I visited Alice in the hospital. She was very pale and pretty as she lay in bed, her big hazel eyes bigger than ever, and her black hair a lovely frame around her small, heart-shaped face.

She took my hand and said, "Oh, Mrs. Shoemaker, how I have wanted to see you and tell you how much you and all those people have done for me. I thought I was going to die and felt so alone, and here I am surrounded by friends. Will you thank them for me? I have been coming to church, but I didn't understand it very well. I think I came to please Anna, but now I know that God is real and that He loves me and that He healed me, and I want to say, 'Thank you,' for the rest of my life."

Alice not only got well, but was married shortly after. The "Faith That Works" group contributed their quarters and dollar bills for a beautiful Bible, which we sent her as a wedding present and reminder of that night of united prayer, when we had all been privileged to share in her healing.

How well I remember some of the people who crowded around me to give their quarter or dollar bill for the Bible—too poor little Negro women, a physiotherapist, an old man who lived alone in a hotel room, a young couple, several office workers, the switchboard operator, a public-school teacher. These people all felt as though Alice belonged to them in a special sense, and they wanted to show their love.

Some time after this a very dearly-loved relative of Alice's was taken ill. Remembering her own experience, Alice wired us, and alerted the minister and people of the church she had gone to as a child. A very large group came together for prayer, and Alice feels that her young relative's life was saved because of it. Alice believes in the power of united prayer, because she has tested it in the test tube of personal experience.

There has grown up among many Christians the false idea that when we pray we must pray alone and in private. True, Jesus said: "When thou prayest, enter into thy closet, and when thou hast shut thy door, pray to thy Father which is in secret; and thy Father which seeth in secret himself shall reward thee openly" (Matthew 6:6). But we have taken this verse out of its context. Here Jesus is inveighing against the show-off, the Pharisee who wanted everyone to know he was a good, prayerful man and took every opportunity to parade his piety in public. In contrast to this is the publican whose prayers are sincere and humble and selfless.

Jesus is not talking against united prayer here, He is talking against fake piety and insincerity and exhibitionism. If He did not believe in united prayer, He would not have urged it on His followers as strongly as He does in the following passage: "Again I say unto you, That if two of you shall agree on earth as touching anything that they shall ask, it shall be done for them of my Father which is in heaven. For where two or three are gathered together in my name, there am I in the midst of them."

In his superb little booklet, *The Secret of Intercession,* Dr. Andrew Murray reminds us of the vital importance of united intercession with these words:

"God's intense longing to bless seems in some sense to be graciously limited by His dependence on the intercession that rises from the earth. . . . God regards intercession as the highest expression of His people's readiness to receive and to yield themselves wholly to the working of His almighty power. Christians need to realize this as their true nobility and their only power with God—the right to claim and expect that God will hear prayer. God rules the world and His Church through the prayers of His people. That God should have made the extension of His kingdom to such a large extent dependent on the faithfulness of His people in prayer is a stupendous mystery and yet an absolute certainty."

A number of modern scholars, Archbishop Temple included, indicate to us that there was a group called a Chabburah Fellowship made up of Jewish men who met on the eve of the Sabbath for spiritual conversation and prayer in preparation for Sabbath worship. According to these scholars, there is every indication that Jesus knew of this fellowship and that it is quite possible that he modeled his small fellowships of the three, the twelve, and the seventy on this ancient Chabburah idea. Archbishop Temple further indicates that Jesus met with his disciples in such a fellowship on the night of the Last Supper, so the idea of prayer in small groups is nothing new. It is as old as the Bible and has been engaged in for several thousand years.

On the night of the Last Supper, when, after an immortal hour of teaching and preparation, Jesus led His disciples in the greatest prayer ever prayed, the High Priestly Prayer of St. John 17.

In this prayer Jesus emphasizes again and again His oneness with His Father, His disciples' oneness with Him, and His and His Father's and His followers' oneness with us. He weaves us all into one united, unbreakable strand.

We can imagine His meetings with His people for prayer and encouragement and fellowship after His resurrection. Then in the Book of Acts we have the record that, in obedience to His command, "these all continued with one accord in prayer and supplication, with the women, and Mary the mother of Jesus, and with his brethren" (Acts 1:14).

Further on we have account after account of the apostles and their converts meeting in secret upper rooms for prayer.

The Service of Morning Prayer in the Anglican Book of Common Prayer closes with the words of St. Chrysostom, Bishop of Constantinople in 398 A.D.:

"Almighty God, who has given us grace at this time with one accord to make our common supplications unto thee; and dost promise that when two or three are gathered together in thy Name thou wilt grant their requests; Fulfil now, O Lord, the desires and petitions of thy servants, as may be most expedient for them; granting us in this world knowledge of thy truth, and in the world to come life everlasting. Amen."

Notice the word "common" and the word "servants." "Common" here means united, and "servants" means us, not me alone.

St. Chrysostom and the writers of the Prayer Book understood very well that the Church was a family, a group of people bound together by a common loyalty to a common Father. They wanted to make sure that no future generations would forget this, so they concluded the service of morning worship with this beautiful corporate intercession.

So group prayer is in the great tradition of the Christian church, instituted by our Lord Himself and carried on by His disciples. The written prayers of the New Testament and the Prayer Book are the crystallization of the free and passionate prayers coming spontaneously from full hearts to the lips of these followers of Christ.

CHAPTER 19

The Value of Family Prayer

There are various ways in which we can pray unitedly. The first way is in the family. The family is the God-ordained group. Most of us have a family, and it is intended, according to the Divine plan, that God should be the central figure of our family life.

Every morning all over the United States millions of doors are opened—black doors, green doors, red doors, white doors, shabby doors, neat doors—and every morning millions of men and women and children stream out through these doors to school, to work, to market. What is in the hearts of all the people from all these homes whose doors open into the world? Is there uneasiness, resentment, fear about the future? Or is there confidence, faith, joy and hope, the hallmarks of a Christian people?

If we were to buttonhole these folk as they hurry past us, I fear the majority of answers would express the first state of mind, and part of the blame would be laid at the feet of the struggling world leaders who, so far, have failed to guide the feet of the world into the ways of peace.

Whatever the cause, this lack of unity, faith, and joy in living reflects itself in the average American family—or perhaps the average American family's lack of these qualities reflects itself in the inharmonious and uneasy state of society at large. We cannot expect a healthy society when, in one year alone, 500,000 divorces were granted in our courts, with the resultant dislocation of children's lives and emotions. As if this were not bad enough, alongside of the broken homes are millions of pagan homes in which a generation of children are being brought up spiritually illiterate, with no understanding of the great moral and spiritual laws that govern all life and therefore no knowledge of how to co-operate with them.

What is the solution? For every problem has a solution. Does it lie in the restoration of a faith that will dignify our existence and give us a cause worth living for? And has the family a part to play in the restoration of this faith?

A family is like a small orchestra. It needs a conductor who will see that each instrument is kept tuned and played in harmony with every other instrument. Then that family will make harmonious sounds within the walls of its own home that will carry out through the doors to the community at large.

The old idea of parental authority seems to be outmoded, but there must be some authority, some final point of reference, or there is no unity. Who, then, is good enough, consistent enough, authoritative enough, to conduct our family orchestra? Who indeed but God Himself? Therefore it is inescapable logic that we should turn back to family prayers and give the Divine Conductor an opportunity to tune us up and draw us together.

Just because some of us carry unpleasant memories of family prayers is no excuse to abandon them altogether. The present lack of any common family discipline or devotion is no adequate substitute for former unrealities. We need to try again. There never has been anything wrong with family prayers, while there may have been much wrong with those conducting them. Let us resolve to be real and humble and believing ourselves, and then family prayers cannot help but succeed.

A real obstacle to family prayer is the bedlam the average American family faces in the early mornings. There is the task of getting the household up; breakfast cooked; the coffee made; Susie and Fred, Jr., ready for school; Fred, Sr., off to work; which altogether is no mean accomplishment, especially if it is to be managed in good order and in good temper.

Let us take a typical American family—Fred and Sue Allen, who live in one of those small, trim, new homes, in a vast new housing development on the edge of a large city. Fred and Sue have decided to experiment with my proposal. So they get up fifteen minutes earlier than usual and ask Susie and Fred, Jr., and Fred's mother, who lives with them, to do the same.

For once, the whole family arrives at the breakfast table simultaneously instead of in relays. Fred picks up the Bible, which has been dusted for the occasion, and reads a passage, after which he proposes a short time of silent prayer so that the passage read may make its particular appeal to each listener. It is surprising how much new truth is continually revealing itself to us in long familiar Bible passages.

Then Fred reads a prayer from that matchless little

booklet, *Prayers New and Old,* or the Book of Common Prayer, or any other manual of prayers, which contains prayers for every mood and every occasion. This draws the family together so that they feel free to ask for prayers for some particular problem or person most on their hearts.

Susie is worried about her school work. Young Fred has a big football game coming up. Fred, Sr., is contemplating a new business venture. Fred's mother has some sick friends. The whole family is concerned about the United Nations and Russia and China, and what the United States should do about the problems they represent.

These prayers are very brief and at the end all join in the Lord's Prayer, or the Apostles' Creed, or St. Francis's great prayer. It does not take more than fifteen minutes, but each member of the family goes through the front door that morning feeling somehow warmed, close to one another, in tune with God, steadied and strengthened, and all deciding in their hearts that they will try to do it every day.

It is one thing to decide something. Who is to carry out the decision? Why, Fred, of course, as the head of the house. So I will give you a few suggestions, Fred, on how to keep the family prayer time fresh and vital.

There are certain things you must keep in mind—worship, praise, intercession, listening, affirmation. Let me emphasize, too, that a few moments of united silence should be a part of every morning prayer time so that the Great Conductor may give to each of us His solution to, or His guidance for, our particular concern. One important warning—don't allow yourselves to become skeptical about what one small unit like yourselves can accomplish.

Remember, you are one of thousands of similar

units spread like a great net across the world. It will thrill your children to realize that they are part of this world family—part of the basic structure of a sound world society. Each little family unit like yours becomes a member of the world family as the prayers of each reach out and fuse with the Great Conductor's creative plan for His world. The Perfect Society is in His mind; it remains for us, His instruments, to play the harmonies that will translate it into actuality—and where better to start than in communion with Him around our breakfast tables? Or, if this is not possible, around our supper tables?

There are three positive results of family prayer that I would like to stress. The first is that every member of a family who consciously and continually turns to "Our Father" for inspiration will find that he or she begins to see the others with new eyes. Where formerly we were critical and resentful of each other's faults, and often blind to our own, we begin to come to a new self-knowledge and a new patience.

We become less aware of the other fellow's sins, and more aware of what we may be doing to contribute to them. In other words, we begin to look at our brother or sister or father or mother-in-law or husband or wife with creative and understanding eyes rather than with critical and resentful eyes. It dawns upon us that if we pray in faith for a different member, little by little a new element comes into the situation, a new hopefulness in us, and in them a new openness of heart toward us and toward God.

The habit of family prayer can create an atmosphere in which problems of growing children are worked out both more intelligently and with less strain on all concerned than usually is the case. Following is the account of the solutions of the schoolwork problem of a fifth-grade child, sent to me by a mother who has always included family prayers as part of the family's day:

"Jane was a straight 'A' pupil for the first three years. In the fourth grade she started to slip, and in the fifth grade she received 'A' in Music and Health only.

"My human reaction was one of disgust, but when I prayed about it, this is the thought that came: 'You often lose your way in trying to do your best, and need help from other people in order to find it again. Jane has lost her way. She does not know how to use her mind. Ask her to write out for you the ways you can help her.' This is what she wrote out:

"1. Make me study every afternoon at 5 o'clock.
"2. Tell me what books to bring home.
"3. Ask me to read a paragraph and then tell you what I have read."

For six weeks her father worked with her. At first the sessions were long and stormy. After three weeks, one half-hour sufficed. After five weeks her card showed marked improvement, and soon after Jane was able to study alone at 5 o'clock. Now, because her work is accurate, she seldom has home work, and her card satisfies parents and teachers.

The praying mother and father turned to God for help with their child; then they made a personal sacrifice to carry out the direction that God gave them, and the problem was solved.

The second positive result of family prayer is a sense of common purpose. We come to realize that we have been placed in our family for a reason. To put it very simply, God has a plan for us as a family. What higher adventure can we imagine than finding the part we are to play in carrying out that plan?

Third, family prayer develops in us a sense of

world citizenship. We learn to live together creatively, we learn to act as a team to meet human need, and we learn to concern ourselves with God's world. Family prayer is the best cure I know for the insular point of view, for racial or national prejudice. The need of the world becomes our concern. Little children have a natural sense of world citizenship, as illustrated by this prayer of a five-year-old child.

"Dear Jesus, please be with all the little children who are hungry, especially the Germans, the Koreans, and the Africans and please make your peace all over them and all over the world."

In one fine American family of my acquaintance the hour for family worship was at the end of dinner in the evening. That seems to be the time when the family is most likely to be assembled.

The father always read a Psalm, then the whole family got down on their knees around the dining table, while the father prayed first for absent members, and then led in the Lord's Prayer or one of our other universal prayers.

This quarter-hour of united worship had been observed since the children were old enough to attend. Most of them are grown and married now, and their babies have joined the circle. No one is asked whether he would care to attend—all are automatically included, guests, new in-laws, anyone who happens to be present.

One of the grown sons tells the story of the time, during World War II, when the oldest boy, who was in the Navy, had been alerted for Okinawa and was sailing at midnight. Another son was at Camp Lejeune, a daughter at college, the youngest son at prep school, and a little sister at home.

The father arranged a telephone hookup at the usual dinner time, and promptly on the dot, with the whole family listening in, he carried them all through the customary service of family worship, including them all in his blessing, especially commending the boy going into battle.

It was a time none of them will ever forget—the familiar voice, the familiar words, the sense of family solidarity, and above all, their common faith in God's all-embracing love and care.

Many years later when this same grown son mentioned in the above story had married my daughter and had felt called to go out to Korea to serve as a medical missionary with the Presbyterian Church, we were gathered in the living room of our home in Pittsburgh for our farewell evening together of family prayer. It was a time of fellowship that we shall never forget because, while we did not know it at the time, my husband was never to see this little family again in this life.

I remember well Court and Sally and their three little boys gathered with us around our dining room table, with our beloved Mamie and Jean, her great-niece who lived with us. It was a cold evening in February, the supper dishes had been moved back, and my husband led us in the great prayers for those we love, those who would be absent from us, those who were going on a journey, and those who would be serving in far countries in the mission of the church. Then he dismissed us all with his blessing, as Court's father had done so many years before when he commended his children who were enlisted in the service of their country to our same great God and Savior.

It gave us a great sense of security and assurance as this little family launched out on their great physical and spiritual adventure into a completely alien culture and nation in the service of their Lord. It helped us to realize, as we had never realized before, the reality of the grace of the great hymn which we sing so often and so lightheartedly in our church services, "Give of Thy Sons to bear the message glorious; Give of Thy wealth to speed them on their way; Pray out thy soul for them in prayer victorious till God shall bring His Kingdom's joyful day." If only the families who are so frequently now separated and spread all over the world knew the secret of keeping together in the fellowship of prayer and in communion of spirit, how much easier it would be not only to endure separations but to realize that there is no separation in Christ Jesus.

If we can get across to our children that sense of the concern of God with the affairs of the whole world, that sense of being channels of His power, I believe that they are not likely to lose it as they go through life.

God is standing outside the doors of our homes—the black doors, the green doors, the red doors, the white doors, the shabby doors, and the neat doors. Shall we open those doors to Him and invite Him into our family circle? He is waiting for us to do just that.[16]

CHAPTER 20

Prayer Groups in the Church

How can the power of united prayer affect a church, and through a church influence a whole community?

In Calvary Church, Pittsburgh, the church in which my husband was rector for ten years, twenty prayer study groups met weekly. Some of them met in the parish house during the day, some of them met during the evening, some of them met in each other's homes, and several men's groups, which eventually emerged into what is now known as *The Pittsburgh Experiment,* met downtown at the lunch hour in various parts of Pittsburgh. These groups were made up of young married women, middle-aged housewives, women who were wheels in the church organizations, women who were active on the hospital and civic boards of all kinds, couples who met in the evenings, and business and professional women who met in the evenings, as well as downtown during the lunch hour.

Underlying all of the dynamic outreach of Calvary Church in Pittsburgh, was the network of small anonymous groups which met together as I have indicated for Bible study, discussions, and intercession. It is significant that while we left Pittsburgh in January, 1962, a number of these groups have faithfully continued to meet. The faithfulness in prayer and study of these small anonymous groups has been a factor in the vital outreach of the parish church.

Each of these groups chose different books of the New Testament for study, rotated its leadership every week and chose its own prayer concerns. There emerged, however, certain united concerns which bound us all together. One was the unity of Christendom, one was world peace, one was racial reconciliation, and one was the needs of the parish and the diocese. Beside this, each of our groups prayed for individuals in every kind of need—breaking homes, sorrow, sickness, and every other calamity that can befall us frail human beings. We were very careful to keep the names of the people for whom we prayed confidential, in fact the members of the group often did not know who they were as we mentioned them only with an initial or a first name. Individuals in all the groups supported our weekly healing service and one wonderful group in particular, a group of elderly women, attended the healing service every Wednesday and supported it with their prayers.

At seven-thirty each morning, for several years, we prayed unitedly for world peace, for our President, for the conversion of Russia, and for our Church.

During one period of time there was a teen-aged child in our parish who was dying of a rare disease, for which as yet medical science has not discovered the cure. The disease induced a spastic condition which affected her speech and the control of her hands and feet. As she became increasingly ill we all agreed that we would pray daily that "God would supply all her needs and that she might be encouraged and strengthened."

The hope that this united support brought to her and her family was wonderful to watch. They all have felt help pouring in hourly. It was a joy to visit that home. The shining, selfless love of the parents and the shining beauty of that child's soul in a weak and helpless body were truly inspiring. You can imagine the effect of this child's radiant courage on all of these new young prayer groups. She herself wrote a beautiful prayer which she sent to each of us:

"Almighty God, my lord, who has brought me safely through the trial of my life and has been my friend, companion and guiding light, I thank Thee for the friends who have been channels of Thy faith, love and courage. I thank Thee for the miracles of Christ which were revealed to me by the ministry of the Church. I pray that I may remember the debt I owe to God and pay it in service to others like me."

This radiant child has gone to meet her "friend, companion and guiding light." If "Life is the anteroom for the great interview with the King," then surely she is standing before Him now.

The parents of this lovely child continued to be tested because not long after her death, her younger sister contracted the same strange rare disease and also died. We were called upon to continue to surround the parents with our prayer concern during this second terrific ordeal. By a miracle of grace and because of their own deeply steady faith, these two wonderful young parents came through the death of their children with a quiet dignity and victory which was an inspiration, not only to the people of our parish and to our prayer groups, but to the whole city.

The mother has since become the headmistress of

one of the large private girls' schools in the city and is being used to serve hundreds of little girls.

It has been a growing conviction of my husband's and mine throughout our ministry, that the great things of the Spirit of God emerge in response to obedience in the small things. Neither my husband nor I claimed to be saints in any sense of the word, but we have learned of the importance of obedience in small things. The first thing I was led to do upon going to Calvary Church, Pittsburgh, was to accept the invitation of the women of the Church to address them on prayer. Out of this emerged the demand for a School of Prayer. Out of this emerged the establishment of this large number of varied prayer groups. Out of this emerged an annual School of Prayer which I held for seven years and which resulted in a great ecumenical Prayer Group Reunion dinner and meeting in September of every year. Then I was led to become Prayer and Worship Chairman of the Third Province of our Church, which consisted of twelve dioceses, and at the suggestion of the wife of one of the bishops of the dioceses we began to think in terms of holding an Annual Prayer Group Conference for Anglicans and any other interested persons who might wish to gather once a year for the lifting of sights and new inspiration and new instruction in the "how" of the ministry of prayer.

Accordingly, we began to hold a series of Prayer Group Conferences which started in 1958, with the Bishop of Coventry, England as our first conductor and which emerged into what is now known as the Anglican Fellowship of Prayer, which has a Board of Advisors, a Statement of Purpose, an Annual Conference, and acts as an increasingly well-known clearing house for those involved in prayer groups, those interested in starting new prayer groups and those engaged in the ministry of prayer all around the world.

All this is based on the Prayer Group activity of one local parish and has emerged out of it in obedience to our Lord's great command: "Go ye into all the world and preach the Gospel," which I should like to paraphrase as, "Go ye into all the world with the ministry of prayer and thus help Him to bring in the Kingdom which is after all the purpose of His Church in the world."

Soon after their groups had begun, the young couples of the parish were put to a real test. The baby son of one of them fell desperately ill with dysentery. Immediately a member of the group telephoned all the others and a prayer chain of special intention was formed. We prayed around the clock for that little one and his parents.

"Prayer is an appeal to the friendship of God. . . . If we are God's friends, and come as such to Him, we must prove ourselves the friends of the needy; God's friendship to us and ours to others go hand in hand. When we come thus we may use the utmost liberty in claiming an answer."[17]

These young people, many of them new to the idea of united intercessory prayer, gave their whole hearts to their intention. The parents of the baby said afterwards that they could feel courage and poise and trust flowing into them, and the baby, who had been so ill that my husband had gone to the hospital for an emergency baptism late at night, suddenly and unpredictably began to get better.

Later the doctor often jokingly referred to the fat, healthy, pink-cheeked cherub that he became as his "miracle baby."

At our first parish prayer group reunion some two hundred persons participated. What spiritual dynamite for a parish! One person spoke for each group, and you may like to read briefly what these people experienced.

The first speaker was a middle-aged woman whose son had fought in the front lines in Korea. Her group was remarkable because six months earlier the members were practically strangers to each other. These women were of different backgrounds, different tastes and different church affiliations, yet all had the same spirit. Here is what she said:

"Here we are twelve people who six months ago were practically strangers—seven from this church and five from others. A number of us had never even met before.

"As the weeks have gone by we have, through fellowship and the medium of prayer, become very close. All masks are off. We are completely ourselves, sincerely and uncritically loving one another. This warmth and concern for each other has been a startling revelation to all of us. It's something that just miraculously happened. Why are we so surprised to find ourselves acting the way God expects us to?

"We all realize that this same wonderful thing can happen to anyone. So, as a future goal, we are going to try to get this knowledge across to others. One of the girls said, 'And to think of what we've been missing all these years!' Her particular resolve is to try to pass this on to her two children, of college age, and to young people generally.

"One of our members finds this little group particularly precious because it's different from all the other things she belongs to. It isn't something we joined because it was the thing to do, or because of the people who belonged. We're all there because we want to be, because we're desperately aware of an emptiness in our lives.

"That is how we feel. . . . Now what have we done?

"We have learned to enjoy the Bible as we never did before. You would think that we had been brought up as heathen who had never known the Bible. Somehow, everything just seems new and different.

"Our meetings have gone along without a definite system of leaders. Someone is always ready and willing to take over. Most of all, we are learning to pray—at the meetings, at home, and when alone. We've found out, too, that praying isn't easy. It demands thought, and our minds are lazy.

"Slowly we're becoming articulate, gaining confidence, losing that almost painful self-consciousness that we had, and I'm sure that here, if in no other place, we come close to true humility—so aware are we of our shortcomings.

"The subjects of our prayers are changing too—more for others, less for ourselves. The emphasis has shifted to God and to larger things. We pray for peace, for our country, other nations, all leaders and all people, the United Nations and the Church Universal.

"One little characteristic of our group is that those who are absent always pray with us, wherever they are, from 10:30 to 11:30 on Thursdays, and of course we pray for them.

"During the last six months of my son's year in Korea, most of which time he was in the front lines, I found strength, courage, and actual tranquillity, knowing that our little group was constantly praying for him. Thursday was always my best day."

Another spokesman, a young husband this time, told what the middle-aged couples group, which met on Thursday nights, had been experiencing:

"The fundamental purpose of our prayer group is to dedicate ourselves to prayer for others and welfare of our Lord's Kingdom. We feel that the prayers of several can be more effective than those of just one alone. We felt from the start that it was necessary to understand the basic elements of prayer, and to endeavor to incorporate these into our prayers.

"Our group consists of six couples who meet regularly every Thursday night. A different moderator is chosen for each meeting to lead the prayer and discussion periods. Our prayer session lasts for about thirty minutes and the discussion for forty-five minutes. During the prayer portion of our program the moderator uses the basic form of Evening Prayer from the Book of Common Prayer, including the prayer for all sorts and conditions of men, and supplements these prayers with others taken from any source. At one point in our service everyone participates by offering his own spontaneous prayer. Such prayers may vary from supplications for a particular person's health to prayers for world peace, the United Nations, our parish, etc.

"For the discussion period we have read the four Gospels, being particularly aware of reference to our Lord's own prayers and instructions which He gave us for praying.

"The value of any such endeavor can be measured only by its accomplishments. We feel that we have learned some of the basic principles of prayer. We feel that we know better how to pray and how to express ourselves.

"As we look back we now recognize that our prayers at the start were quite narrow in scope. Today they are not only supplications, but they express thanks and praise to God.

"We feel that the Christian fellowship of our group has helped us all. The fact that we know we will be understood by everyone is quite reassuring. We find that we are more willing to talk about God and prayer to others among whom we would not have mentioned the subject previously. Since ours is a couples group, many discussions of the subject have developed at home—a good influence on each of us individually, and on our entire families.

"We believe we have become more objective in our outlook on life in general and more sympathetic to the views and opinions of others. Most important of all is a greater recognition of God's presence at all times, and a greater appreciation of the power of prayer."

These are only two reports of the twelve who reported that memorable evening. The others were equally individual and powerful. A parish is indeed blessed when it is permeated with such prayer power.

Again to quote Andrew Murray: "Who can say what power a church can develop and experience if it gave itself to the work of prayer day and night for the coming of the kingdom?"[18]

If every church, not just a few churches in this great country of ours, were releasing creative spiritual energy into the bloodstream of our country through the kind of prayer Mr. Andrew Murray describes, who can foretell what kind of hope and leadership the United States might give to the world?

CHAPTER 21

Prayer Groups in the Community

Do not allow a prayer group to become an escape from taking sacrificial, responsible action. A prayer group is not an ivory tower into which we can retreat from the necessity of grasping the nettle. United prayer never fails to lead to some kind of constructive action. It seems to sharpen and focus all of our faculties, and we are led to do things which ordinarily we would never think of doing.

In November, 1952, a member of our parish, an instrument man in the Homestead Plant of the United States Steel Company, had the idea that small groups of men meeting together for prayer in various parts of the plant would make for better human relations as well as for better working relations in the plant. He figured that this would not only help his fellow workers in their personal lives but would reduce friction and increase output for the company.

His idea caught on. By December of 1952 a large group was meeting; by June, 1953, another was added. In September the *Pittsburgh Press* felt it of enough significance to publish a story, and in October, 1953, *Fortune* magazine included it in a feature called "Business Men On Their Knees."

If you have ever visited a great steel plant you may appreciate the daring and drama involved in any attempt to meet for prayer in one of the half-mile-long open hearthsheds lined with great furnaces filled with white-hot molten metal. There is the constant noise of furnaces being filled or others being tapped and pouring out great streams of burning liquid into huge ladles. These, in turn, are tipped into twelve-foot molds, which overflow with golden flames and showers of sparks.

There is the clash and clang of the rolling mills, where the enormous red hot hunks of steel are rolled out and cut up into the desired width and thickness, amidst sizzling jets of steam.

There are the tool and instrument shops and the huge loading sheds, where giant hooks are continually lifting, piling, and sorting enormous flat finished squares and oblongs of cold, blue steel, and loading them onto freight cars for shipment.

The following is Dave's account of how these men, in these unlikely places, have proceeded with their prayer meetings and what has happened:

"The original Homestead group, which was started in November, 1952, has continued to met every Thursday morning in the Pyrometer Room of the Power and Fuel Department, using sometimes a tape-recorded talk or sermonette written by ministers of various faiths or by laymen, or often a talk by one of the group.

"Stanley, a Roman Catholic, father of five children, and a top-rated instrument man, decided to build himself a telescope, which he took with him when he visited friends, and while they looked at the heavens through his handiwork he told them what he had learned about the stars and the glory of God. He did a lot of good with his telescope, and one day came to me and said he would like to make a recording, telling the group how he felt about God.

"For Stan this took a lot of gumption, because he was quite shy. However, he made a fine recording and the story was retold later in many other parts of the mill by instrument men who had heard it that morning. Stan has become one of the pillars of the program.

"Matt, the water inspector for the Homestead Works, is a leader in the Pyrometer Room. In addition to his everyday tasks at the mill, Matt has devoted a great deal of time to the prayer program and the spiritual needs of the men in the mill. His talks and prayers on Thursday mornings have been inspired, especially one which was recorded recently. As the men went about the mill repairing instruments they told others about the wonderful story they had heard that morning. As the news spread, there came requests for a copy of Matt's talk. They came from the open hearth, the rolling mills, the maintenance shops, the various offices and even from men working on the railroad which serves the plant. A plant policeman stopped me as I left the plant three weeks later and asked me if I could possibly get him a copy of the talk.

"Matt has given out about four hundred mimeographed copies and is still getting requests for more. As a result of the programs and Matt's part in them, envelopes containing request for prayer have been left on his desk, and they still appear.

"A very good-looking man who had lost what little faith he did have in three years at a too-strict church college has found a new concept of God and life as a result of the program. Tony worked with me for four months and we found time to talk together about God, and at the last to pray together about our individual and collective problems.

"One Wednesday morning, after working all night in the open hearth, Tony climbed into my car and went with me to Latrobe to visit the plant of the Stupakoff Ceramic and Manufacturing Company and heard their morning prayer program, 'Meditation Moments at Stupakoff.' He got some sleep as we drove home but it wasn't until 2 P.M. that I delivered a very tired but happy young fuel engineer to his wife. Tony is now a vestryman in his church, and his reborn faith guides his family life, his mill activities, and I believe plays a great part in vestry meetings.

"Tony told me one morning about 1:30 A.M. that he felt he should talk to the men some Thursday morning. I suggested several topics, but he said he had his own and I had better wait and see what came of it. He held the men enthralled with the story of what God had come to mean to him and his family.

"Henry, a machinist, started to pray about what he might do to bring God and faith to Homestead. Three days later, after talking to many of his fellow workmen, he initiated a prayer group in one corner of the balcony of Number One Machine Shop. Sixteen men gathered at 7:45 A.M., fifteen minutes before starting time, to hear Henry, a solidly built, gray-haired German who came to this country after World War I, read from the Bible and pray. Henry's group has continued to meet every Wednesday morning from 7:45 until 8:00 A.M.

"Another young man, Chuck, has taken hold of the idea of brotherly love and putting Christianity to work in our everyday life by actually going out in the mill and talking and showing men what God has come to mean to him. He has reorganized a defunct Men's Club at his church and has had six meetings. The membership covers the entire range of ages, and in their meetings they are studying the fundamental aspects of the church.

"A number of very bad domestic situations have been happily resolved. Confusion and indecision in the minds of many men have been cleared up, and the knowledge has been firmly implanted in the general consciousness of people all over the plant that God hears our prayers, that prayer is the key to all situations, and that we can love and understand our fellow men."

From a steel plant in Pittsburgh we cross a continent and an ocean to the Island of Formosa, where another remarkable prayer experience is taking place.

Not long ago a most remarkable document arrived in the mail of a United States senator. It was entitled, "A Resume of Our Year of Evangelistic Work of the Chinese Christian Women's Prayer Group," which came from Taipeh, Taiwan (Formosa). It described the five-member women's prayer group formed by Mme. Chiang Kai-shek soon after her return to Formosa in January, 1950. Their purpose was to stimulate all Christian women in Formosa to pray earnestly and devotedly for a spiritual revival among the women of Formosa and China, so that they might become spiritually equipped to reform society and build new homes in a new China.

Every Wednesday these women met for prayer, opened by a period of Bible study. Out of this group emerged five family prayer groups, three family Bible classes, and four Sunday Schools numbering four hundred and fifty children, as well as twenty centers of Christian work. From it also came a committee to organize an evangelistic program and establish chaplains in six army hospitals, where three thousand wounded have been reached and twenty thousand soldiers have heard the Gospel. The members of the prayer group have visited the hospitals, and at Christmas saw to it that there were Christmas trees and gifts for the men in every ward.

Over eleven hundred people were baptized as a result of this spirited action, and two touching stories are told of the help brought to wounded men. One man who had lost the power of speech was converted, and spoke immediately. Four young officers who were badly wounded and suffering great pain had agreed to commit suicide, but after hearing the chaplain preach, they turned their bottle of poison over to him and were baptized instead.

In 1965 I had the privilege of meeting and talking with Mme. Chiang Kai-shek in the United States. I asked her if her prayer group movement had prospered and with shining eyes she told me that the vision of the original small group was being realized and that a spiritual revival was truly taking place in the lives of thousands of women on Formosa.

Group prayer sets up a positive chain reaction of which no one can forsee the end. Whether we meet as a family or in prayer study groups, or meet in prayer, though not in person, "for special intentions," where two of us agree to pray secretly for some particular concern, or meet at the altar rail, the result is always the same—power is released, people are healed and changed, hope is reborn, and above all, we do our small share in fulfilling Jesus' vision: "That they all may be one; as Thou, Father, art in me, and I in thee, that they also may be one in us: that the world may believe that thou has sent me" (John 17:21).

The prayers and efforts of fifteen to twenty employed Christian businessmen in Pittsburgh alone have resulted in approximately four hundred men finding employment over a three year period. Most of the men found their own jobs as their experiments in prayer brought about increased confidence and a renewed faith in God's love and concern. Others found work through leads provided by those men who were employed.

One of the leaders of *Employment Anonymous* tells his typical story: "As we met at lunch with unemployed men, we found that they often had something more than just an employment problem. They had lost initiative, aggressiveness and confidence in themselves, and certainly had lost faith in their God. We encouraged them to try prayer, and some of them embarked on a thirty-day prayer experiment. We suggested that they pray each day for thirty days that God would give them the will to work. This seemed to change many of the men and they found a new confidence, a new faith, and went out with a new attitude.

"At later meetings they reported that when they went for interviews they seemed to be better received, and undoubtedly made a better impression. A number of 'success stories' tended to re-invigorate the men who were still looking for work. Those who first found employment would come back to the meeting the next week, tell of their experiences, and testify to the power of prayer and the change it had made in their lives.

"One man said that he had left the first meeting and had begun to pray regularly that he would find a job. Sometime later, when preparing for his daily period of prayer, he stopped a moment and said to himself, 'Mel, you've just been praying for work. Perhaps it's time to pray that the Lord will strengthen your faith.' The next day the phone rang, and a man who had interviewed him some weeks before asked if he was still looking for employment. And the following day he went to work.

"Hearing a story like that gave new courage and faith to men who had thought their problem insoluble. One man who had been unemployed for eight months started on a thirty-day prayer experiment to ask for the Lord's help for his situation, and twenty days later went to work in a position better than he had even hoped for. He was so convinced that prayer was the answer that he started an unemployed neighbor on a similar prayer program, and prayed with him for help in his situation. The neighbor went to work just twenty-nine days later.

"The amazing thing about all of these cases was that the job each man found fit his qualifications perfectly. The coincidences which occurred could only have been the work of the Lord in answer to prayer. None of the men who have tried to help in this work are trained in employment or personnel work, and we have no magic formula. We tried to open any doors we could and contacted people around the city to let them know of these men in need of work. The results which occurred, however, were far beyond our limited means, and came for the most part from changes in the men themselves."

Prayer in a steel plant in Pittsburgh . . . Prayer among the women of Formosa . . . Prayer between employed and unemployed men in a large city. . . .

A friend in Canada wrote me just the other day to describe the results of the meeting and praying together of six clergy and their wives: "This may seem very small, ordinary and not at all earth-shaking. But there is nothing earth-shaking about a blade of grass, and grass covers the habitable earth."

It was St. Paul who said "Do you not know that the saints are to manage the world?" (1 Corinthians 6:2, Moffatt). Who are the saints? The workers in a steel plant . . . Chinese women on an island in the Pacific . . . business men on their knees.

CHAPTER 22

The How of Prayer Groups

If you have read this far in this book, many of you, at this point, will ask the question: "I agree that prayer groups and participation in united prayer are biblical, desirable, valuable and even essential for the renewal of the church and the building of the Kingdom, but how can I start one in my own church or my own community?"

I will outline some of the ways in which we could go about starting and continuing with prayer groups. I will begin with a talk my husband gave at a prayer conference in Pittsburgh in 1963 in which he made some very concrete suggestions about prayer groups: how to start them, how to continue with them, some of their dangers, as well as the need for them and the value of them:

"In a business or factory or office, two people in spiritual fellowship have much more effect than the effect of either of them multiplied by two. It is a different kind of impact, not possible by isolated individuals even in large numbers, but only by more than one in actual and living fellowship.

"But the part we are more concerned about is the 'two being agreed as to anything they shall ask, and it being done for them of my Father which is in heaven.' Here seems to be no groping prayer nor seeking of God's will, but rather a testimony that if two people discover some person or situation about which they feel common concern, and put their minds and prayers on the person or situation, and keep them there, what they ask will be granted. What this points to, obviously, is that much more power is released by united than by single prayer. We must remember that this surely has nothing to do with being a better way to gain God's attention, or anything whatever in the nature of a 'gimmick.' It must mean that in such laws as govern prayer and its answer in God's universe there is more responsibility and more of a channel opened for God's power to use than in any single prayer. It seems to me impossible for us to do more than get into a metaphysical discussion about why this is true, when actually we do not know why it is true. But through experience we may come to know that it is true. Whether the radiations from just two people multiply much more widely than from just one, or just how the power is released, I do not know. But I know the peculiar power of a group of people, united in their intention, constant in their intercession. The answers to prayer poured out in united power for individual members of prayer groups or for someone else outside them, or through intercession at Holy Communion, are too numerous to need more than a reminder of them. Any of us here could probably enumerate ten or twenty of them. If God designs to work in this way, let us not ask questions. Let us rather pray in the way Jesus told us to pray.

"We might now remind ourselves of some of the uses of a prayer group:

"1. Its first use is for the release of this kind of power in the direction of people and situations which have called out our concern.

"2. A second use is for fellowship and inspiration and mutual help. We find that neither our problems nor our failures nor our victories are peculiar to ourselves, but we are dealing here with something universal and therefore are finding out more of what it means to be a human being.

"3. A third use is for spiritual growth. In such groups we learn better how to pray. We learn more of the fundamental content of the faith, by getting our theology with and through experience rather than instead of experience. And we learn how to be articulate about our faith: if we cannot make it clear what we mean in such a company of like-minded intimates, how on earth can we ever be convincing to people outside?

"4. A fourth use is: finding ammunition for the spiritual warfare. We all have met people who know a lot of theology and a lot about the church, who are hopeless in the presence of a pagan—say the wrong thing, bring up arguments he would not for a moment accept, prove that they live in some outer-space of an ecclesiastical or theological world all their own. Genuine spiritual experience, our own or that of others told in simple earthy kind of language, is the only thing that will convince him. And here you hear first-hand stories about contemporary people, the kind that live on your street, which are inescapably convincing.

"5. This leads on to the fifth use of these small groups: training in helping other people to find faith.

As it is impossible in the Christian life to act without praying, I think it impossible also to pray without acting. This is not to say that sometimes prayer is not the best action you can take, for it is; but many times we are meant to take responsibility as well as to pray. And learning about God's ways with people we shall become less and less immature in dealing with human situations.

"We may well look also at three dangers of such groups.

"1. The first is an exclusive congeniality. I don't see why we shouldn't enjoy each other increasingly in such a company, but when it is anything like a club, there is something the matter with it. If it contains attractive and well-known people, and is known about, there may be some climbers who would seek status by joining it. Let us beware of this, and suggest they form their own prayer group, as we had to do with ours. But let us watch any kind of real exclusiveness.

"2. Second, we must take care not to fall into ingrowingness and self-absorption. We can get more and more concerned about less and less.

"3. And of course the third great danger for any who seek to step out even a little beyond the majority is self-righteousness. Now and then God gives all of us spiritual influence and spiritual success. What we say and do, helps people and they tell us so. And if we aren't careful it goes to our heads. I must say I do not see how anybody can retain this feeling very long; because we must know that any power we have was given us from God, and there must be enough failures and set-backs to keep us from any very permanent self-satisfaction. People look for this in articulately religious people, and so we must guard against it all the time. You may know the story of the Carthusian monk who was describing characteristics of some of the great Catholic orders: the Dominicans were famous for their intellect, and the Franciscans for their simplicity, but he said: 'When it comes to humility, we Carthusians are tops.' Let us watch for these dangers, and yet never let the possibility of them swerve us from our work in and through the small, praying fellowships.

"Let us for a moment enumerate a few of the things that help in forming and continuing them.

"1. There is great value in having a small core of concerned people from the first, so that the group is not too much colored by one person, though often the faith and persistence of one person is what carries it through.

"2. Second, it will help to be regular, setting aside faithfully the time for the meeting each week and holding by it with some stubbornness and what William James called 'cruelty to the lesser claims.'

"3. Third, the study of the books will help fill it with body and content—books of the Bible first—one thinks of St. John and Acts especially—but then great books on prayer or spiritual experience. Don't let study be an 'out' for responsible action—let it contribute to action.

"4. Fourth, there are some small mundane things, like having a well-lighted, well-aired room, coming on time and ending on time, so that people can build the time into their other responsibilities, and the meeting does not drag into talk and time-wasting.

"5. A fifth thing is varying and changing leadership. These are training groups, really, and people are not trained by watching others except at the beginning; they must begin taking on leadership themselves.

"6. The sixth thing is that these groups will span the wide distances between personal and public concerns. Some begin personally and end up with their hearts on the international situation and the world;

others, the other way around. The more we know and the better read we are on public events, the more specifically can we pray. Such a small, intimate group may be an introduction to a concrete world-wide concern. Praying for the world's leaders by name, for situations specifically mentioned, seems part of it, as does praying either by name or by situation for individuals—not often for both because it may reveal confidences that should be kept; and to this end we need practice in controlling our tongues lest something that began as sacred trust, wind up in very unsacred gossip.

"7. When all is said and done, it appears that we have found in the small groups what Dr. Chad Walsh once called 'the missing link between public worship and the private spiritual life of believers.' We have, by emphasizing only public worship and private prayer, created a whole generation of inarticulate, immature believers. The small group, where prayer and expression and experience may come into the open, is training thousands and tens of thousands of people in becoming more mature, more knowledgeable and more responsible.

"I close with some words from St. Augustine: 'Without God, we cannot. Without us, God will not.'"

Earlier I described the work of the wife of an Episcopal rector in the Diocese of Los Angeles, Mrs. J. Herbert Smith. She has also given us some very helpful suggestions in regard to prayer groups as a result of her experience with them in her own parish and diocese:

"The forming of a prayer group and what takes place in one comes through the guidance of the Holy Spirit. Christ is the Leader. We are the channels. No two groups are alike any more than two people are. The emphasis and procedure is worked out depending on the need and the conviction of the group. Sometimes a group may feel led to pray for peace, another one to pray regularly for a particular project (such as one in the East which prayed for the abolition of the horrible conditions in a mental hospital, with the tangible result that reform was begun). Other groups pray for the sick; some combine prayer and study, spending a half-hour on each.

"A Prayer Group could best be defined as an organic association with other people whose center is Christ—a living organism and not an organization in the ordinary sense of the word. People of all interests and types are drawn together into a convinced, concerned, committed fellowship. Those who participate have a sense of vocation about intercessory prayer—namely, prayer for others, that they may be healed in body, mind or spirit, or all three. A group may meet in a home, a parish house or a church. Some prayer groups number three; others as many as twenty people. The ideal size is twelve, the number of the disciples chosen by our Lord.

"What actually happens in a Prayer Group? There is no final pattern. It is more like a laboratory or a spiritual refueling center through which the laws of the spirit are tested and tried on the anvil of life itself. At the start there is always the mood of Adoration—where one waits to feel the Presence of Christ in our midst. The Bible is read. Helpful thoughts which have grown out of one's personal devotional life, or through the reading of some book, may be shared. There is always a time of living silence when one gives oneself to listening prayer, so that one may hear 'the still small voice' of God Himself. There is opportunity for communication where individuals may share the wonder of answered prayer or the name of a person facing special need like surgery, or the necessity of wisdom for some major project undertaken. If confidences are occasionally shared with a Prayer

Group they must be kept in the spirit in which they are given. The most important part of the hour together is the time of corporate prayer for the church, the nation and the world, and more particularly for their leaders who carry such heavy responsibilities. Some people pray aloud. Some silently. What feels sincere and real is always the thing to do. The time together usually closes with the Lord's Prayer.

"What are some of the results of belonging to a Prayer Group? Once we have prayed with a person and not just for him or her, no relationship is ever the same again. Deep ties of fellowship in Christ have been forged which go deeper than the finest in human friendship which we have known. Secondly, the iron curtains of our often self-centered and self-contained lives are leveled through the love, understanding and insight of those with whom we meet. We can do more corporately than we can possibly do alone. Thirdly, we see 20th century miracles in the lives of people as their spiritual potential is released. Fourthly, we become more articulate about matters of faith and Christian experience and have an increasing desire to bring other people to a life of power through Christ. Finally, due to this regular association with a group, we keep our major objectives in focus and learn how to 'put first things first.' To be in a Prayer Group is not like 'joining' one more group like the PTA or the Garden Club, but is the great overarch which strengthens all the girders which extend from and support the arch.

"Prayer Groups are islands of peace and of hope amid our confused and turbulent world. They strengthen our association with our church and add a new force to our corporate prayer each Sunday morning as we say together, 'We bless thee for our creation, preservation and all the blessings of this life, but above all, for thine inestimable love in the redemption of the world by our Lord Jesus Christ.' He it is who is the great beginning and the great end of every Prayer Group."[19]

Following are suggestions for Prayer Groups By Mrs. Smith:

"1. Rotate your leadership each year. This trains more people and the group is not dependent on one person. The one taking ultimate responsibility for notices, details, or phoning others to pray for someone who is sick or in need, may also ask another in the group to share the leadership at a particular meeting.

"2. Promptness. This should be looked at as an act of unselfishness to others.

"3. Length of meeting. An hour or an hour and fifteen minutes is adequate.

"4. Frequency. Weekly or bi-monthly, depending on the conviction of the particular Prayer Group.

"5. Priority. When we include new people, put it in that framework—a must except for illness or absence from town—not another activity like the Garden Club, P.T.A., etc. If it is just another activity in a person's mind, then she is not ready for a Prayer Group.

"6. Inclusiveness. A Prayer Group cannot be based on affinity and exclusiveness, even though we may humanly enjoy being with some people more than with others. Prayer cuts across all conventional lines and social groupings. People are drawn to each other by the guidance of the Holy Spirit. He is no respecter of persons.

"In forming new prayer groups, the main thing is to meet a need and put people where they have natural ties and freedom to grow—might be ties of interest or age or prayer projects that have drawn them together for a time.

"7. Strained Relations. They sometimes existed in the early church between Christians. If any exist in your group, set about rebuilding the bridge. We often allow frictions to develop between each other, tend to judge and talk too critically to others rather than praying and talking it out with the persons involved, in honesty and love.

"8. Prayer Groups complement and deepen our relationship to all else in the church. They are no substitute for our central act of worship in the Holy Communion, for Sunday morning Worship, for attendance and participation in other church activities which are channels through which we can show our love and concern for others, and primarily our love for God. Prayer Groups help to train us in informal worship and in learning how to pray with power.

"9. Procedure. This is the work and guidance of the Holy Spirit. No two groups are just alike any more than two people are. The answer will come through prayer and the need of the group. The need may change from time to time so the procedure must be flexible.

"Sometimes a Prayer Group is just for prayer and silence and pooling the rich experience of 20th century miracles in people and situations.

"At other times a Prayer Group can combine Bible study or the study of a religious book for half an hour, with a half hour of intercession and meditation.

"We, like the disciples of old, are still asking—'Lord, teach us to pray.'

"Some suggestions for intercession which include prayer for the world, the church, others and ourselves. (Each group should ask for guidance as to who and what to pray for.)

"PRAYER FOR WORLD LEADERS

The President
The Secretary of State
The United Nations leaders
Heads of Government throughout the world.

"PRAYER FOR CHURCH LEADERS

For the Presiding Bishop (Superintendent, convention president, or whatever your denominational head is titled)

The Bishop of your Diocese (those who superintend the state or area work of your denomination)

The Clergy of your local church, including the church staff

The President of the Episcopal church women both locally and in the Diocese (W.S.C.S., or W. M. U. or whatever your denominational women's work is entitled)

Missionaries to whom your church gives

Young men studying for the ministry

The professors in our Seminaries

"PRAYER FOR WORLD AND NATIONAL NEEDS

Peace

Desegregation in our country and in South Africa

Delinquency of children and parents

Drug addiction

Alcoholism

Church unity

Deepened worship emphasis in our women's organizations

"PRAYER FOR THOSE IN NEED

The sick, the bereaved, those with personal problems.

For ourselves that we may be dedicated enough to be powerful channels in His service.

"10. Communication. A time of talking over the good news of Christ at work in us, in people we know, in situations and in our needy world. The confidences of others must be kept with the greatest of care. The power of Pentecost—'He is risen'—needs to come more and more into our touch with each other in prayer groups.

"11. Closing Prayer. Always have a closing prayer

said by one of the group or all join in the Lord's Prayer.

"12. In forming prayer groups always consult your rector or pastor."

We will cull from these suggestions for those who wish to engage in group prayer the procedures which apply best to our need—the need of our group—and fit in best with the prayer ministry to which our Lord is calling us, keeping in mind that prayer *unites* above all denominational differences. It is our great unquestioned common denominator, and the one ministry in which we can all engage together.

CHAPTER 23

The Power of United Worship

The late Archbishop Temple says: "The world will be saved by only one thing, and that is worship." Dr. Nels Ferré says, "A praying church is a worshipping church, a worshipping church is a working church."

The World Day of Prayer is held on the first Friday of Lent by women in ninety nations throughout the world, and is in a sense symbolic of the power of the praying and worshipping church. Imagine on this day, from sunrise to sunset, women around the world gathering in kraals, grass huts, forest glades, chapels, and cathedrals to offer their prayers of praise and petition to their living Lord!

In 1949, for the first time, a World Day of Prayer service was held in the great Marienkirche in the Soviet sector of Berlin. An eyewitness sent the following moving account:

"Today I have had an experience which I shall

probably never have again in my lifetime, and I must tell you about it. . . . First you must come to Berlin, to the doors of the Marienkirche. . . .

"This is the *Weltgebetstag der Frauen,* the World Day of Prayer for Women. Four years ago such a world prayer day was unknown in Germany, and then Mrs. Arthur Siebans, the wife of the pastor of the American Church in Berlin, arrived. She felt that this movement, world-wide, should find a place also in this great city. From very humble beginnings, together with only a few German women, she organized the first *Weltgebetstag der Frauen.*

"As we drove here from our home in the American sector, we saw a sign—'You are now entering the British sector of Berlin,' and then another—'You are now leaving the British sector of Berlin.' That meant we were entering the Russian sector of Berlin. . . . Because we shall park outside the church, we feel rather safe in taking our car today. We would not park outside a private dwelling, it might be too dangerous for the people within.

"The Marienkirche is perhaps the largest church in Berlin. It has a very long nave and a deep chancel. Partly destroyed during the war, it has been somewhat restored and whitewashed within. It is very beautiful.

"And yet we cannot go through the doors before you know something more, for coming right out of America you have not yet felt the fear which is here in the east sector and in the east zone. First you should hear the words of a fine young Christian who said to me: 'Fear crowds in upon us; it fills our days and our nights, and when you are hungry and cold, and dare not speak, it is hard to keep hope alive in the heart.'

"And then you should also know something about the women who lead today's prayer service. It is too dangerous to name them. All of them have suffered. Most of them have husbands who resisted during the Nazi times. All of them today are giving their lives to help their brethren.

"Now you and I enter the little anteroom off from the church hall, where we who take part in this service bow our heads and pray for God's blessings. Then the wonderful organ music begins and we quietly walk up to the front of the church through the long aisles, past the packed pews, trying to overcome the emotions which crowd upon us as we see this great old church, newly restored, whitewashed, full to overflowing with three thousand women!

"Are you standing beside me? Can you see them, these women, drably dressed, white-faced with tired eyes, many standing because there are not enough places to sit in this cold, unheated church, and each of them here to pray! We know that all the world over, today, 'from the rising of the sun to the going down thereof,' women are gathering in churches to pray for peace. . . .

"First we pray for forgiveness for the sins of not caring about our brother, for waiting for peace to come from somewhere else and not seeking it by having Christ in our hearts. Then we pray for our churches, our brethren, the poor, the sick, the fearful. Then we pray for our world in its great distress, and through all the prayers we pray for Christ to be our personal friend and Saviour, realizing that He gives peace. . . .

"Two women choirs sing beautifully, and then it is time for the meditation and prayers. Now we rise to sing *Ein Feste Burg Ist Unser Gott* (A Mighty Fortress Is Our God), and we know in faith that these prayers can be answered. . . .

"Outside the rain is falling, and the women in their thin old shoes start home to cheerless rooms, black, clammy bread, and no heat. We have brought a friend with us, a woman who has suffered unbelievably during the war years. She sits in the car beside us as we drive her to the Alexanderplatz station and weeps. 'Thank you for letting me come with you. It was to be in heaven! To think there are still that many people who pray, that there are still good men in the world. Truly, this is for me a Holy Day. God bless you!' "

Could this possibly be one of the secrets of the spiritual strength and courage of the people of East Berlin—for this great service of worship is but the outward and visible sign of the secret spirit of worship kept alive in thousands of individual hearts throughout the whole world, and especially in those nations in which Communism has sought to extinguish it.

We all need to become part of the corporate worship of the Church of the world. We sing, "Like a Mighty Army Moves the Church of God," but how many of us join that army so that it may become truly mighty?

If Archbishop Temple is right, and I believe he is, the supreme purpose of the Church is to foster this spirit of worship so that the world may be saved. This cannot happen, however, so long as we refuse to take part in the total life of the Church, the heart of which is worship.

Our Christian faith is the dynamic of our democracy. The precious freedoms which we Americans so much enjoy are the flowers springing from the root of our Christian faith. Neglect the root, and the flowers soon will wither and die. If you refuse to water the root of faith by failing to go to church and joining with others in worship you are in real danger of being one of those giving lip service to democracy while refusing to make it live.

Imagine the towns and cities of this great nation with no church spires piercing our blue skies, no place to go to have our babies baptized, our marriages blessed, our dead buried. This could happen here. It is happening with frightening speed in other lands. The Church could be destroyed. It is lukewarm, indifferent, undisciplined Christians who will sell it out, if ever it is sold out.

I am persuaded that if the majority of our millions of non-churchgoers knew what the Church has contributed to our civilization, what it stands for in the present and offers us in the future, they would enroll in its ranks.

What has the Christian Church contributed to civilization? First, it has been loyal to its founder, the Lord Jesus Christ. Through a turbulent two thousand years of history there have always been those in the church who truly worshipped and enshrined Him in their hearts. As a result, faith in Him and His real meaning for mankind has been kept bright and shining. The Church has nurtured and cultivated the worship of Him, His Father, and His Holy Spirit. In the services of the Church Year the great events of His life and death—the resurrection, ascension, and Pentecost—have been dramatized. In the season of Advent we prepare to receive Him. At Christmas we re-enact, in carols and pageantry and story, the tender accounts of His nativity. In Epiphany we re-enact His early years. In Lent we observe the forty days of His fasting, temptation, and prayer, followed by the climactic drama of Holy Week, when we follow Him into Jerusalem, to the Garden of Gethsemane, and up to Calvary, until we stand before the empty tomb on Easter morning. Then come the Ascension season and Pentecost, the commemoration of the birthday of the Church, when His Living Holy Spirit came into His followers and His Church was born. The long Trinity season reminds us continually of the three-fold function of God. He is our Father, our Redeemer, and our Empowerer. The sweep of this mighty drama of redemption is re-enacted for us every single year in the weekly worship services of the Church, and has been for two thousand unbroken years.

As we come to Morning Worship shall we remember with gratitude, that the Church has not allowed one iota of this glory to be forgotten or fade from man's memory?

Second, the Church has kept alive the spirit of worship in the world. But what is worship?

Worship is a candle in the act of being lighted.

Worship is the soul standing silent before the mysteries.

Worship is an eager heart seeking for the love that never fails.

The world would be poor indeed without the great oratories and anthems by Bach, Gounod, Handel, Mozart, Beethoven, Tchaikovsky, and a host of others, whose gift of music has found its most inspired expression in those paeans of love and praise to their Lord and King.

Our Protestant hymns, which express all our spiritual moods, were written by men whose experience of life and suffering and death have been transformed through worship into songs of triumph.

Such songs and hymns as "Dear Lord and Father of Mankind," "God of our Fathers," "For All the Saints," and "A Mighty Fortress Is Our God" are the heritage of the nations. They are a part of the life blood of worship.

Imagine a world without the great cathedrals of Europe—expressions in exquisitely carved stone and jewel-like glass of the spirit of worship of the men and women of the Middle Ages.

Imagine our civilization denied the glorious religious art and poetry of medieval times and the Renaissance. All of this creative expression was the way in which the artists and poets of that day worshipped. The "Sistine Madonna," the Sistine Chapel, the frescoes of Giotto, the paintings of Fra Angelico, the "Last Supper" of Leonardo da Vinci, the matchless madonnas of Flanders, the poetry of Dante would never have been bequeathed to us if the gifts of these great geniuses had not been their expression of worship.

Our modern system of education was born in the hearts of worshipping sons of the Church. In the Middle Ages the light of learning was jealously guarded in the monasteries, and flowered in the great medieval universities of Bologne, Paris, and Padua. Every one of the great private colleges and schools in our own country was founded by some worshipping son of the Church. Christian education went hand in hand with evangelism in the establishment of our American Christian culture. Most of our universities were founded and established by churchmen.

Wherever the light of learning and literacy has gone in the world, worshipping Christians almost always have preceded it. The Christian colleges of Asia and the Near East are among the most powerful bulwarks against Communism in those lands.

The Church likewise has pioneered the social services. Hospitals for the care of the sick have been brought into being by churchmen, and in the Eastern countries were manned and supported by people who worshipped God through this sacrificial means.

It was a Quakeress, Elizabeth Fry, who with intrepid courage broke through the prejudices and ignorance of early nineteenth-century England regarding prisons and prison life, and became the mother of modern prison reform.

It was a Swiss Protestant and devoted churchman

who felt called of God to plant the seeds of the Red Cross—the only international institution dedicated to the alleviation of human distress.

All of our great networks of social services, all our government agencies to care for the aged, the poor, and the sick, gained their original impetus from little bands of church people who said their prayers and then sought in their own communities to follow the example of Christ in helping those no one else would help.

Modern psychology had its birth in the Church. One of Jesus' greatest acts was the casting out of devils —in other words, the healing of the mentally ill. The early services of the Church contained special services of worship for the mentally ill.

Such is the worship of the Church and the result of that worship. We should be so proud of our Christian heritage, so grateful to our spiritual forebears, out of whose blood, toil, sweat, and tears have come this great gift known as Christian civilization, that we should seek to carry on this great heritage from sheer gratitude! For we are the inheritors of the spiritual experience, the spiritual power, the spiritual heroism, the spiritual creativity and worship of four thousand years of history.

We Americans have a strong sense of family. Many people in this country are justly proud of their ancestors, their family traditions, their family customs, their family's contribution to the building of this country.

The Church is our Christian family. It preserves the records of our Christian family tree. Our manners, our customs, even our common, everyday expressions have been bequeathed to us by our spiritual forebears in the Church. The genius of the Christian family, the romance of the Christian family, the great deeds of the Christian family, are all preserved and carried on for us by the Church. When we go to church to worship together we realize with a deep sense of joy and security that we are part of a great, living company who through the centuries have come together as we are coming together, to worship a living God, not a dead ideal.

What do you do when you go to church? Do you really participate in its service, or are you merely a spectator Christian? Why not try an experiment? Next Sunday try to participate in every part of the service. Sing the hymns with your whole heart, give your full attention to the Scriptures as you read them. Pray silently with the minister as he prays, and, above all, pray for him as he preaches. In other words, enter in and worship! Bring your prayer list with you—the sick, the troubled; bring your worries and fears, and as you worship with all those others you will feel the peace of God stealing in and the power of God giving you new vigor and confidence. You will hear the word of God with new ears, and read the words of God with new understanding. If you really participated in this Sunday worship you would begin to understand all that it means; you might even find that it sets a new pace not only for your week but for your life.

If you are experiencing sorrow or sickness, fear or insecurity, if you do not know where to turn or where to go, come to the church. Go in, kneel down in the quietness of it as millions have done before you. God will meet you there, and take your hand and lift you up as He has done for desperate and heartsick men and women down through the centuries. He will put you in touch with His people, who will give you the comfort and love and fellowship and sense of belonging that you need.

There is a beautiful stained-glass window in the chancel of a church in a great city. Each exquisite medallion of this window tells the story of Jesus' birth, and underneath, in letters of crimson and blue, on a shield of gold, are etched the words: "I am come that they might have life, and that they might have it more abundantly" (John 10:10).

Into this chancel, lighted by the glorious windows, a young man and woman came, hand in hand, to kneel before the altar and take part in the Lord's Supper. It was Christmas Eve. The church was filled with the haunting, remembered refrains of the age-old Christmas carols celebrating the birth of Christ.

These two had come, not long before, out of the masses of gay, attractive, irresponsible young pagans to seek a living faith. Like millions of others, they were appalled and frightened by the insecurity of our chaotic world. Their lives, filled with friends, pleasure, material success, were strangely empty. They knew instinctively that something was missing.

Quite by chance they met a Christian minister who had something. In fact, he not only had something, he knew Someone. Someone who he assured them held all the answers to the questions that were bothering them. The young couple did not quite understand what he meant, but they trusted him. The day they met him the minister had asked them to come to church on Christmas Eve, and here they were.

In the beauty and tenderness of the glorious service of worship they suddenly felt the realness of the Person whose birthday was being celebrated. They felt, too, the nearly overwhelming reality of the millions of average people like themselves, who through the ages had thronged to the great cathedrals, the tiny village churches, to celebrate His birthday and join the shepherds and the wise men in honoring Him. Among these millions there must have been many like themselves who were in need of help and guidance.

After the service, they sought out the minister and timidly asked him if he would kneel at the altar with them for a few moments. The three of them came forward, and in the dark, warm chancel, beautiful with the candlelight throwing into relief a statue of Christ with His arms outstretched, the young couple simply and haltingly pledged to Him their loyalty, and asked Him if He would allow them to become part of His family.

That evening they knew for the first time the meaning of the words inscribed underneath the Nativity window. Suddenly they felt free, with a glorious, tingling freedom, as crisp and sparkling as the brilliant December night. They felt, too, that they had found a family, that they had found a Person whom they could worship, and a cause to which they could whole-heartedly give their loyalty, and entrust their lives.

Nailed to the main doorway of a lovely colonial church set on a hilltop in the rolling farm country of Maryland, is an invitation that is half a prayer:

"Friend, you have come to this church.
No man entering a house ignores Him who dwells in it.
This is the House of God. He is here.
Pray, then, to Him who loves you and awaits your greeting.
Give thanks for those who in past ages built this place to His glory.
And for those who dying that we might live have preserved for us our heritage.
Ask that we who now live may build the spiritual fabric of the nation in truth, beauty and goodness.
And as we draw near the Father through our Lord Jesus Christ,
May we draw near to one another in brotherhood."

CHAPTER 24

Conclusion

This little book is a trumpet call to faith and action. In it we have taken a fearless look at the terrifying world and the personal forces which are threatening our freedom, our happiness, our lives.

I do not believe that Communism or total mutual destruction are the wave of the future.

We hope that this book will inspire you to join us, the great growing army of God's people who believe that nothing is too hard for Him, and that with Him as our leader, we will prove that spiritual force is still the first force in the world, and that Our Lord's vision, "Thy Kingdom Come," is not an empty dream, but a glorious possibility.

Dr. Fritz Kunkel, the well-known psychotherapist, says, "Watching the religious development of our time, no one can say that this is the agony of a dying faith. It looks more like a beginning. Christianity, it seems, is coming of age. It might prove to be the decisive factor in the future of mankind. That Christianity will finally conquer the earth is certain, and every real Christian will participate in this success even though he may actually perish in a concentration camp."

We, the people of prayer, may feel very small and ineffective as we face the potential destructive power of evil, and yet Jesus' promise is to us, as it was to His handful of trembling disciples on the hills of Galilee, "Fear not little flock, it is your Father's good pleasure to give you the kingdom."

Acknowledgments

1. Dr. E. Stanley Jones, *The Way to Power and Poise,* Abingdon Press, New York and Nashville, Tennessee.
2. Used by permission of Dr. Theodore Ferris, Rector, Trinity Church, Boston.
3. Father George, *God's Underground,* Appleton-Century Crofts, New York City.
4. Dr. Elton Trueblood, *The Life We Prize,* Harper & Brothers, New York City.
5. Ibid.
6. J. B. Phillips, *The Young Church In Action,* The Macmillan Company, New York City.
7. Dr. William Temple, *Reading in St. John's Gospel,* St. Martin's Press, New York City.
8. Dr. E. Stanley Jones, op. cit.
9. Dr. William Temple, op. cit.
10. Ibid.
11. Harry F. Gerecke, "I Walked to the Gallows with the Nazi Chiefs," *Saturday Evening Post* (Sept. 1, 1951), p. 17.
12. Dr. William Temple, op. cit.
13. Dr. Norman Vincent Peale, *The Power of Positive Thinking,* Prentice-Hall, New York City.
14. Ibid.
15. "Faith That Works," *The Calvary Evangel,* New York City.
16. Ibid.
17. Andrew Murray, *With Christ in the School of Prayer,* Fleming H. Revell Co., Westwood, New Jersey.

18. Ibid.
19. Alys B. Smith, *Why Parish Prayer Groups? Their Purpose and Power*, Episcopal Churchwomen, Los Angeles, California.
20. Dr. William Temple, op. cit.